GIVE YOUR DREAM A PLAN

7 Questions to Ignite Extraordinary Results in Your Business

Barbara J Richards

VisionWork Publications
3406 Lynmoor Place
Vancouver, British Columbia V5S 4G4

Cover art and book design by
Linda Naiman, CreativityatWork.com

Library and Archives Canada Cataloguing in Publication

Richards, Barbara J., 1952-
Give your dream a plan : 7 questions to ignite extraordinary
results in your business / Barbara J. Richards.

ISBN 978-0-9876819-0-4

1. New business enterprises. 2. Business planning.
3. Success in business. 4. Businesswomen. 5. Self-realization. I. Title.

HD62.5.R53 2011   658.1'1   C2011-904380-7

Printed simultaneously in the United States and Canada.

Dedication

To Jim Spence, my father and first business mentor ("Treat the customers well. Remember, they put the food on our table today.") who showed me daily that business can be a vehicle for living our spiritual values and touching people profoundly.

CONTENTS

6. SO, HOW IS THIS GOING TO HAPPEN?

7. WHO IS THIS CALLING ME TO BECOME?

LIVING YOUR VISIONPLAN

Introduction

"What do you really want?
If you could design your business
exactly the way you want,
what would you create?"

That's what I recently asked Marie, a Personal Chef who came to me for advice on how to grow her business. We were sitting at a small table at the back of a crowded neighbourhood pub. The conversation was electric as she shared her dreams for her personal cheffing business. Suddenly, she became quiet. "You know, sometimes I wonder if I can make it with this business. I'm on fire with possibilities, but feel like I'm running in all directions at once. I'm swamped with urgent demands, and don't know where to start with these ideas." I could hear the sparks of her dream, but knew that if we didn't breathe some life into them immediately they were at risk of being extinguished.

What is your dream for your business? Whether you are a seasoned veteran or a new entrepreneur, there's always a sense of possibility aching to be expressed. But quite likely, just as with Marie, the sparks of your dream are in danger of fizzling out. Your days are spent doing busy work. You now have a 6–or even 7-day work week. You're working harder than ever, but much of your time is spent doing things you don't like. When you do get some free time, you're too burned out to enjoy it. This definitely wasn't the plan.

So where did the dream go? Is this just the hard reality of being self-employed? Are all the naysayers right when they say people can't make a successful business out of their dream?

They couldn't be more wrong! The most successful businesses are built on dreams and passion (just ask Steve Jobs and Anita Roddick). Your dream is still there. It just got stuck under a crushing pile of details, and without a plan for moving forward that's where it will stay. To make sure that doesn't happen, you have to re-awaken your vision, connect with the life you want to author, and devise a strategy that will allow you the time and freedom to turn your dream into reality.

Planning in a Radically New Way

Love it or hate it, a plan will make the difference between your business dream staying a fantasy, or becoming your new life. But for most of us creative entrepreneurs, just hearing the words "business plan" makes our eyes glaze over. Why is that? What makes planning such a struggle?

Think about it for a moment. When you hear the word "planning" what springs to mind? Tedious meetings? Stacks of paper written in business-ese that only makes sense to an accountant? Something cast in concrete that just doesn't have anything to do with real life? Traditional planning tends to be heavy, complex and simply too constrictive for us creative entrepreneurs. Add to that the reality of a rapidly changing marketplace that means traditional plans are usually obsolete before they're finished. Even when we've taken the time to create a plan quite likely it ended up in a file drawer never to be used. No wonder we dread it.

What you need is something radically different. A living plan. One that focuses your ideas, ignites your intuition and motivates you to take immediate action with enthusiasm. One that's simple, that guides your actions and can be adjusted quickly in response to changing conditions in the market place.

Over many years of coaching passion-business owners – small business owners, doing what they love for a living, and making a difference that matters—I've developed a simple, flexible and integrated process for taking the deepest desires for a business and turning them into a roadmap to success. I wrote this book to teach readers the same steps my clients have taken with great success. As you go through these pages, you're going to learn that process and create a framework that captures the essence of your business ideas.

7 Questions That Ignite Extraordinary Results

Most books about business planning miss out on what it really takes to succeed. Typical planning focuses on what we want (our vision and concrete goals) and how we'll do it (our strategies and actions). But to accomplish our dream these alone aren't enough, no matter how well they're defined.

There is a third essential dimension that makes the difference between failure and extraordinary results: You. Achieving your deepest desires for your business depends on who you are. It means finding your essence, transforming resistance and building on who you are deep down inside. When you do, you tap into an energy that will take you where you're meant to go.

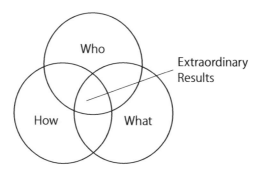

The seven questions we'll use in this book unlock the power of each of these essential dimensions. You'll look in depth at what you want most for your life and your business. You'll discover your natural and effective ways of how to accomplish this. And most importantly, you'll tap into who you are and harness ways to express your authentic self more fully as you grow a business you will love. Working with this three-pronged approach—What, How and Who—is the key to igniting extraordinary results.

Chapter by chapter you'll engage the power of each question and apply it to your business. Answering them will unlock your passion, harness your ideas, give shape to your vision and guide your actions every step of the way. Here's a quick preview:

1. What is my passion? Know and orient your business around your brilliance.

The primary question for fulfilling business success is, "What do you do best and love to do?" You're hard-wired to do something very well. It's where you shine, and how you naturally add value to others. You'll uncover your "something special" and make it the cornerstone of your business.

2. What kind of life do I want to author? Start first by developing your life vision.

Your business is meant to serve your life, but for this to happen it means you need to know what's most important to you. You'll pinpoint your life priorities, which will put your business in perspective and ensure you're going in the direction of happiness.

3. What do I really want in my business? Develop your business vision, based on the Real You.

This is your business. You get to design it exactly the way you want. You'll paint a picture of your business two to three years from now, when you're singing your song and your business is thriving. Tapping into your inspiring vision immediately energizes your present, and unlocks new creative thinking.

4. What is my True North? Unleash the power of purpose.

Your business is an extension of your self. It is totally unique. There has never been a business like this before in history and there never will be again. Your business purpose captures and communicates this uniqueness. You'll develop a simple, inspiring statement that motivates you and speaks directly to your best clients, the people you are meant to serve, whose needs are a perfect fit for your brilliance and your company's mission.

5. What's my definition of success this year? Craft your top goals.

A year from now, what do you most want to be celebrating? New clients? New services? Higher revenues? You'll put legs under your business vision by pinpointing your most important goals that spell success now.

6. So...how's this going to happen? Map out your game plan.

Success is rarely an accident. It's the fruit of a compelling and doable game plan. You'll craft your core, passionate business-building strategies that give shape to how you'll accomplish your dream. Then you'll design 90-day action projects that launch you into doable actions and produce immediate results. Finally, you'll ground your dream in a financial plan that's a blueprint for a flourishing and profitable business.

7. Who is this calling me to become? Achieving your vision takes learning and growth.

The difference between success and failure is you, who you will be. An inspiring vision calls us to become more than we are right now. It means being who you are deep down inside and growing beyond your normal zone of comfort. Personal transformation is the most exciting part of being a passion-business owner. When we dare to dream, we dare ourselves to step up to a new level of our greatness.

These seven questions will guide you in creating a VisionPlan for your business dream and will empower you to step out boldly to make your dream a living reality.

How to Get the Most from This Book

If you're stalled out, stuck or struggling with your business dream, I'll bet it's not due to lack of information. There's an abundance of information on building successful businesses available on the internet or in bookstores. The trick is applying what you know, taking active steps toward your goals. Action is the answer, and support is the key.

As you read through these pages, I'd like you to consider me your personal executive coach, here to support you in the business of your business. You've probably experienced the positive impact of working with a coach in some area of your life (sports, drama, sales). Growing your passion-business is another place where coaching can help you achieve extraordinary success.

Early in my career I experienced the power of coaching with one of my passions, acting. I worked with world- class acting coaches who helped me understand my talents (and limitations!), showed me how to bring out the best in my performances and overcome obstacles like stage fright. They challenged me to set high goals based on a clear knowledge of my abilities, and stood beside me celebrating my successes and urging me to stretch even further. In the same way, a business coach can help bring out your best and guide you to grow a fulfilling and successful business.

I've coached hundreds of people to move into action. As your coach, I'll be a blend of consultant, mentor, cheerleader, sounding board and support system all rolled into one. Often I'll remind you of the things you already know, but haven't yet integrated into your life. I'll motivate and challenge you to think differently, to take risks and try new things. I'll teach you simple, effective business skills. You'll learn how to constantly improve your game, even when that means going back to re-learn the basics, and re-design your plan.

Each step of the way, I'll be beside you cheering you on. I know first-hand what you may be going through. I love being an entrepreneur, but I also know how challenging it can be. I recognize what it's like to work in today's high-paced, competitive, ever-changing marketplace. I understand the stress a small business can put upon your personal life and relationships. I also know what it takes to create a profitable business that supports your life priorities. I have consistently earned a good livelihood doing my passion for over ten years. I've grown a business that is aligned with my deepest commitments, becomes more satisfying and prosperous each year, and provides my clients with high levels of satisfaction.

Each chapter will have many opportunities for you to apply the ideas and tools you'll be learning in own business. If you are willing to work hard, invest some time and energy in this process and take a few acceptable risks, I guarantee your business—and your life—will change dramatically. You'll put yourself in charge of making your vision become your reality. You'll pull your dream out from where it's buried, shake off the critics (both inside and out) and make a living doing what you love.

I want you to have a business that achieves your dream. As I write this, I am championing your efforts and celebrating each new skill you master and every authentic risk you take.

I'd love to hear your success stories or questions as you develop and live your VisionPlan. Please feel free to send me an email at barbara@ visionworkcoaching.com or share them with me on my blog at www. visionworkcoaching.com/blog. I'd love to post your successes (of course with your permission) to inspire others to follow their business dream and learn from your successes.

 YOUR TURN—Starting Out

The first thing I want you to do is get a notebook for your VisionPlan work. This week, get a lined notebook or a binder specifically for our work together. Throughout the book you'll have questions and activities to help you reflect, gather ideas and map out your plan.

To get started, take out your pen and write your first entry on these questions. Write a page or two, letting your thoughts flow freely.

- What do you most want from reading this book?
- What's the current situation of your business? What challenges are you facing?
- Without taking long to think about it, what's your dream?
- When you think of creating a plan for your dream, what comes to mind?
- What do you want to change, resolve or accomplish that would make your dream come alive over the next few weeks?

If just thinking about boldly stating what you want in your business is a bit daunting, relax. We'll take this step-by-step. Your vision is just under the surface waiting to come out. You have everything you need to get started and just by engaging in these questions you'll start to feel a new energy, inspiration and motivation very soon.

Now, let's get started with the first of the seven questions—What's your passion?

WHAT'S MY PASSION?

What Is My Passion?

"What in your life are you brilliant at?
In your heart you know what you do best."
—Jennifer White

"I think I'm in the wrong business." Jessica, a successful self-employed investment advisor for over seven years, was discouraged and frustrated. She went on to say, "I'm unhappy every day when I go to work. I've felt stuck for months. I'm really torn, because I've invested so much in building up my business, but I can't keep going on like this. Something's got to change."

"Tell me more," I said.

"I'm working harder than I ever have, but I'm not getting ahead. I've got ideas about ways to let people know about my services, but I struggle to do anything with them. I've been feeling like the odd-person out in this industry for a long time now. Maybe I'm just in the wrong business and need to make a change."

While it was possible that Jessica did need to make a radical change, I had an inkling that something else was going on. I'd heard these symptoms many times before. Successful, but unhappy. Working more hours, but not making more money. Highly skilled, but feeling second best. Many ideas, but unmotivated. Busy chasing opportunities, but unfulfilled.

Whether I am speaking to a seasoned veteran who has hit the doldrums with her dream or a new entrepreneur who is just launching out, I've learned that these signals usually point to one cause. I followed my hunch and asked the question:

"Jessica, what is it you do best and love to do?"

I heard her take a breath. Then silence.

The question had hit the mark. I knew she had not yet answered the primary question for fulfilling business success. Who are you, really? What is your passion? Our number one job as business owners is to discover our passion and then organize our business so that we are doing that most of the time. Over the next few pages you'll see how Jessica took on this vitally important task, pinpointed her real passion and found the essential ingredient to creating a remarkable business.

What Is Passion?

Each one of us is born with the ability to be great at something (or several things). We are hard-wired from birth with unique gifts and they cry out for us to use them. We use many different words to describe this. Passion. Brilliance. Genius. Bliss. Joy. Our calling. What we are meant to do.

Whatever we call it, we recognize it when we feel it. It's that sense of being connected to the spark, the flame, our inner light of being, our authentic self. We were born to use this passion. When we do, life sparkles. Our inner flame burns brightly. We have a compelling sense of direction, boundless energy and unstoppable motivation.

The secret to a thriving and fulfilling business lies in identifying your passion and putting it to work at the heart of your business. Happy, successful, satisfied women business owners I meet know where their talents lie and build a business and life that expresses their passion best. To grow a business you love, one that's sustainable and has endless possibilities, you must

1) discover what you do best,

2) work increasingly at mastering it,

3) present it in a way that appeals to your audience, and

4) do more and more of it in your business.

Imagine, what would your business and your life would be like if you did what you do best and love doing 80 per cent of your day?

But, Isn't Passion a Luxury In Tough Economic Times?

Marie, who we met in the first chapter, had been an accomplished Human Resources professional before being 'downsized' in a major corporate merger. We were meeting to explore her options for the future, and when I asked her about her passion she stopped short. "You know, for the past few months, since the layoffs started, I've been daydreaming about what I might do if I were let go. I've had a fantasy for years to start my own business as a Personal Chef. But, I couldn't do that now. I couldn't become self-employed during this economic slowdown. I have to do something more practical, don't I?"

She'd put her finger on one of the biggest obstacles our passion has to face. During difficult economic times, popular wisdom tells us to take the safe, secure path. Do what others are doing. Follow what the experts say is the hottest, surest trend. We hear a constant barrage of messages from the media, colleagues, loved ones, consultants, and teachers, telling us to forget our unique ideas and get "practical." That thinking stops most of us from understanding, valuing and searching inside for our true potential.

The fact is, popular wisdom in this case is dead wrong. Knowing and leveraging your passion is especially important in the midst of uncertain economic times. Rather than being an indulgence or a luxury, it is your greatest personal resource for creating a solid, sustainable future. Understanding your real brilliance will give you a highly practical tool for developing a business that is remarkable.

It's when we don't orient around our passion that we put ourselves at risk. There can be a profound cost to not letting our passion lead. We become vulnerable to chasing the hottest trend even if it's a mismatch to our talents. We become swamped by the options because we don't have a trustworthy compass for decision-making. Our business becomes a pale imitation of what others say is the best way to succeed. We become increasingly unhappy, unsuccessful, uncertain and we earn below our potential.

It takes courage to fly in the face of conventional thinking and choose to put your passion first. But when you do, you'll tap into your true power.

✍ *YOUR TURN—What Could Stop You from Trusting Your Passion?*

You have a unique passion within you. If you find it difficult to iden-tify and own what you do best, you are not alone. As I've coached hundreds of women to orient around their brilliance, I've heard many common issues. We haven't been taught how to recognize what we do best and love to do. In fact, most of us have probably been taught not to be guided by our passion. We've been told to fit in, not rock the boat. When we've dared to say we have gifts, we've been told not to become "too big for our britches" or that pursuing our passions is childish and self-indulgent.

What messages could be keeping you from understanding and valuing your passion? What have you heard from parents, col-leagues or the media that may be submerging your natural passions and causing self-doubt? List the most common reasons you've heard against following your passion.

_____

_____

_____

_____

_____

As you read this chapter, continue to watch for messages that could prevent you from fully embracing your truest passion. Jot them down as a starting point to freeing yourself of their debilitating grip. You will find these reasons aren't yours, but someone else's assumptions.

Passion Pays Real Dividends

Knowing and orienting around your brilliance isn't childish, self-indulgent or a luxury. It's your number one job. When you do, the dividends will be substantial:

You will avoid chasing the hottest trends when they are a mismatch to your talent. Rather than being drawn into a hot fad, you'll have the clarity to make tough decisions. You'll know whether you are following a true urge that will lead to what you are meant to do, or getting swept up in someone else's desire.

You will be positioned to make the contribution you're meant to make. You'll have an unshakable knowledge of your best product—you—before you even approach your market. You'll know your best way to make a unique, positive, profound and lasting impact on the world. As you learn to harness your natural talents, new pathways to success will open up, and you'll become highly attractive to the people you want to service.

Knowing and deeply trusting your passion will give you courage and confidence. Of course, the challenges of business don't simply disappear once you let your passion lead. In fact, sometimes the opportunities you're drawn to when following your passion will be even scarier and stretch you further than anything you've done before. But when you're living your passion, you tap into a sustainable power that both energizes you with a sense of purpose and makes overcoming daunting challenges worthwhile.

Even during uncertain economic times, understanding your real brilliance gives you a highly practical tool for developing a business that is remarkable.

Which brings us to a practical question. How exactly do we discover what we do best and love to do?

Pinpoint Your Passion

"What you love is what you
are gifted at. There is no exception."
—*Barbara Sher*

What do you do best and love to do? What's your passion? As a business owner, you probably have a good sense of your brilliance. Whether you've "just always known," discovered it through working with a coach, or just stumbled onto it you quite likely have a good sense of what you do best.

Now, I want you to take it a step further. I want you to pinpoint your passion and make it the cornerstone of your business. I want you to know it to your bones so that it fuels you and guides your business evolution for the rest of your life. When you do, you'll put yourself on a path for limitless success.

How do we recognize our passion? Our soul's code is sending clear signals every moment of every day. We each have a built-in guidance system that, once understood, provides clues to what we do best. We know we are using our passion when we:

Feel energized and 'lit up';

Experience moments of flow, lose track of time and are in the 'zone';

Learn something quickly and have a fascination for it;
Yearn to be doing something and feel discontent until we can;
Hear other people notice and value this about us.

Your passion has been with you throughout your life, but it may be in deep hiding from the negative messages you've received. Over the next few pages I will give you three simple, sure-fire ways to tap into a direct experience of your passion. First, you'll ignite your inner guidance system and learn to recognize passion clues. Next, you'll look at some of your sweetest moments to understand what you do best and value most. Then you'll include others in your passion search to get a clearer picture of how you uniquely contribute to others. Finally, you'll name and claim your essence in a way that starts to transform your business and life immediately. Then, over the course of the rest of this book these insights will provide the underlying compass settings for all aspects of your business. While most business books focus on techniques, information and other external sources, we are first focusing internally— identifying your passion— before designing your strategies for success.

Ignite Your Inner Guidance System

There is a powerful secret that has helped hundreds of women business owners I work with pinpoint their uniqueness. We turn on our inner guidance system by asking two simple questions:

What energizes me?
What drains me?

Simple, but profound. By tuning into what energizes and lights you up, you'll quickly recognize what you naturally do best. Equally, by listening to what depletes you, what irks you or weighs you down, you'll understand what you need to stop doing in your business, or delegate to others.

At first, when Jessica heard these questions, she was a bit puzzled. "I'm not sure I'd recognize what energizes or drains me," she said. "My entire day feels hard at the moment."

"I understand, Jessica, but I'm sure as you use these questions you'll be surprised. Just start by noticing as you go through your day what energizes you and what depletes you. When you get a burst of energy, stop what you're doing and write it down. Conversely when something feels wearisome, write that down too. I want you to get very specific. As you gather clues, write them in your journal and bring them to our next meeting."

A week later, she reported with enthusiasm. "A light bulb went on this week. I hadn't seen this before. There is a definite pattern about what makes me feel heavy, tired and irritated, and what I enjoy. When I'm analyzing stock, doing research or preparing reports for my clients I feel like I want to run from the room screaming. I can't sit still. But, when I'm talking to clients, especially when I'm helping them understand investment strategies I feel fantastic. I could do it for hours."

Let's dive into using these questions to uncover clues about your most enlivening passions.

 YOUR TURN—*Ignite Your Inner Guidance System*

Turn to a fresh page in your VisionPlan journal and draw a vertical line down the centre of the page. At the top of one column write "Energizes Me." At the top of the other put "Depletes Me."

Reflect back over your day or week, and think of times when you felt fully alive. On fire. In the flow. What were you doing? Make a note of it in the "Energizes Me" column. As well, think of times when you felt heavy, irritated, mired in mud. What was happening? What task or activity felt so draining that you wanted to run from the room screaming? Make a note of these in the "Depletes Me" column.

Energizes Me	Depletes Me
_____	_____
_____	_____
_____	_____
_____	_____
_____	_____

For example, Jessica's lists looked like this:

Energizes Me	Depletes Me
Talking to clients about anything	Analyzing stocks
Teaching concepts about investing	Preparing computer reports
Answering client questions	Making fast decisions about buying and selling stocks
Designing a long-term financial well-being plan	Learning new computer programs
Talking to clients about anything.	
Teaching concepts about investing	
Answering client questions	
Designing a long-term financial well-being plan	

As you go through your work day stop periodically and ask yourself, "Is what I'm doing right now stimulating me? Is it lighting me up or draining me?" Take stock of as many of your key business tasks as you can. When you notice an energizer or an irritant, add it to your list. The more concrete and specific you can get, the more potent these clues will be in understanding your real passions. For now, simply observe. Don't jump to conclusions, or make judgments about what this might mean, just gather clues. Soon you'll be using these to understand what you do best.

Mine Your Sweetest Accomplishments

Your most meaningful moments can provide rich clues about your passion. The second way we'll pin point your brilliance is to reflect on some of your sweetest accomplishments in your business, unearth passion clues, and discover what they say about what matters most to you.

When Jessica thought back over the past year, two accomplishments quickly surfaced. "One of the highlights of the past year was developing a presentation on investing and giving the talk to the residents at my mother's independent living community. Another was taking extra time with one of my older clients to explain a few investment strategies in depth. Afterwards, when she sent me a note saying that she now understands things and feels in charge of her financial future, I glowed with satisfaction."

"What could this be saying about your passionate abilities? What matters to you?" I asked.

She became quiet. Finally she said, "I've always felt odd and different from most stock brokers I know. The other advisors are so much faster with their clients than I am. I want to take the time to educate and explain things to my clients. What if I'm not 'slow'? What if giving careful guidance is my passion? That would change everything." She'd pinpointed and claimed her passion. It was a turning point in revisioning her business. Jessica felt a sense of calm and confidence she'd never felt before.

YOUR TURN — Your Sweetest Accomplishments

Take out your pen and VisionPlan notebook, make a cup of tea (or anything else that sooths you) and set aside an hour to reflect on your business. You may want to take some time to get in a quiet place so you can really concentrate. At the top of the page, write "My Sweetest Accomplishments."

Now, take a deep breath, go to your heart and without giving this much analysis, think over the past few months or year. What have you accomplished that you feel pleased about? What has occurred in your business that matters most to you? What makes you smile when you think of it?

It might be something that occurred recently, or it might have happened a while ago. It might be a high-profile, public accomplishment involving the accolades of others. Or it could be a private, low-key victory. What matters is that it's meaningful to you. Try to jot down three or more of your sweetest accomplishments in your notebook, and write a few lines describing what happened and what makes it stand out for you. Then, reflect on them to see what they may be saying about your passion.

What was I doing in each accomplishment that I love to do?

_____

_____

_____

_____

What makes these meaningful to me?

_____

_____

_____

_____

Soon we'll use these clues to define your unique contribution.

Ask Others

One of the biggest challenges most of us face in our passion search is recognizing what we do best. Our brilliance is second nature to us which makes it almost impossible to see. When we include others in our search, we get a much clearer picture of our true passionate abilities.

You see, passion doesn't exist in a vacuum. Our brilliance only comes alive in relation to others. It's what connects us to the people who need our unique contribution. Our clients come to us for a particular reason. They're attracted to us and work with us because of the way we reach and empower them. One of the best ways to uncover clues about our passionate abilities is to ask them what they value most about us.

In this section, I'm going to ask you to go and get positive feedback from your clients. Including clients in your passion search by asking what they appreciate about you will yield quick and very useful insights.

I know, this can be a little scary. When I gave this assignment to one client, her face went blank. I suspect she was remembering earlier times when she opened up for feedback and heard comments that were less than kind. If those memories are springing to mind, relax. We're going to do it differently this time. There is a way to elicit useful information and minimize those awkward reactions. You'll be choosing clients who are your best supporters, setting the stage so that you gain new insights into what you and your services bring to others that really matters to them.

When Jessica asked a few clients she was delightfully surprised. They were touched that she'd asked and their comments confirmed what she already begun to suspect was her uniqueness.

"You take time to explain things to me. No one else ever has before."

"I don't ever feel stupid around you. No question is too small."

"I really feel that you care about my future. I'm not alone in figuring out what I need for retirement."

✎ *YOUR TURN—Ask Others*

First, chose three to five clients who are your best supporters. They might even be raving fans. They appreciate your work. They want you to succeed and they will probably be delighted that you're asking for their support. Pause now and jot down who you would like to ask and decide when you will contact them.

Who   When I could contact

_____   _____

_____   _____

_____   _____

_____   _____

_____   _____

Set up a time to talk with them by phone or in person (this is not a time to use email). Tell them you are doing a little research as part of enhancing your services and would like their input. Ask them what they see as the gifts you have. Be sure they understand you want real feedback, not praise or flattery.

Now, here's the key. Remain curious, and ask the question a few times (of course, in different ways to keep it interesting to them!) The 'gold' we're looking for only comes out after a few minutes. Keep listening and probing and soon you'll hear what you, your services and business bring that really matters to them.

After you have had a conversation and heard their feedback write their comments in your notebook.

Client Feedback: *Where do your clients and supporters feel your brilliance the most? What do they say is your unique contribution to them?*

_____

_____

_____

_____

Now, if just the thought of asking your clients for feedback is making your stomach turn and your palms sweat, I understand. This can feel intimidating (on both sides!). Here's an alternative. Recall what people have said to you or leaf through your files to find letters of recommendation, impact statements or thank you letters. Scan them, and pull out the comments that most make you smile. Often our clients' spontaneous expressions of praise and gratitude give us the best insights into what people see in us that we just can't quite see in ourselves.

Name and Claim Your Essence

By now you've gathered many clues about your passion. It's time to distill them all into a simple phrase that captures who you really are.

This is perhaps one of the toughest questions we've looked at so far, but once you catch the idea, it will crystallize what you do best and love to do. It will give you a simple way to describe the core of who you are. It's important to capture and anchor this so that you can reconnect with it any time you want to. This is your inner compass, and we'll use it throughout the rest of this book to shape and direct all aspects of your life and business.

We will start by looking back through all the clues you've gathered, this time taking stock of who you were being when you've felt most energized, fully alive and when you've touched people in a way they genuinely value.

When Jessica reread her energy clues, looked over her sweetest accomplishments, and reflected on what her clients said they valued most, she initially felt like she was wandering through thick fog. The question of who she was being was truly baffling. We bounced ideas back and forth and soon a new way of viewing herself opened up.

"I'm beginning to see what you're saying, especially when I think about my sweetest accomplishments. When I designed and gave the presentation on investing to my Mom's friends and when I took time to explain concepts to my clients, I was being the same thing: A guiding light. It might sound kind of corny, but that's who I was being. In fact, that is really meaningful to me. When I'm being my authentic self, that's it. I'm a guiding light."

She had named and claimed her essence. It had been there all along, but she hadn't seen it because she was focused somewhere else. Now that Jessica had pinpointed her passion—in a way we could say her purpose—she immediately felt different about herself, her business and her future.

 YOUR TURN—*Name and Claim Your Essence*

Turn to the clues you've gathered in your passion search activities and look at them with a fresh eye. As you read through them, ask yourself, "Who was I being in this experience?"

You are looking for the essence of you. You might capture it in a phrase, a metaphor or an image. Let your intuition guide you. You're looking for the natural built-in talent you give to the world, just by being who you are. It's always been there. It's how you impact people. It's how you make a unique and valued contribution.

When you have a sense of your essence, write it here:

I am _____

_____

If you're feeling a bit baffled yourself by this question, don't get discouraged. Articulating your brilliance can be a challenge. It's tough to be objective with ourselves with something that's so close to us. In fact, your essence is beyond words. The phrase you're creating is simply a way to describe the core of who you are. We want to capture and anchor your insight about your unique passion in a phrase so that you can reconnect with it any time. But realize it's about the feeling, the big picture, not the specific words you use.

If you've glimpsed your essence, you now have a fundamental awareness about yourself that's probably changing you already. Quite likely you are feeling differently about your life, your business and your future. But, this new clarity alone isn't enough to make a lasting difference. There is another critical step you'll need to take to unleash the full power of your passion.

Unleash the Full Power
of Your Passion

*The pursuit of mastery...has become
essential in making one's way in today's
economy. —Daniel Pink*

Congratulations! If you've worked through these activities and named your passion, you've done tremendous work. You have answered the most important question in life and in your business—who are you, really?

Very few people consider themselves unique, and fewer still try to define their uniqueness. You've done some powerful work in understanding, claiming and valuing your greatest asset. You've harnessed a force for growing a remarkable and successful business.

But, this self-awareness alone isn't a magic bullet. Claiming your real passion is the first step. However there's another equally important step needed to unleash the full power of your brilliance and attract endless possibilities.

You'll need to invest in your brilliance and become a master at your craft.

Yes. A master.

Think of Oprah. She had a great gift for communication, connecting people with information and motivating change. But she didn't just rely on her natural talent. She became a master at it. Not only did she become a competent talk show host, she changed the game. She constantly tried new approaches, took risks by going down new paths, listened for trends before they could be heard by most, and broke the mold in her industry.

Masters first learn the basics of their craft or industry. They understand what it takes to be competent but they aren't satisfied with just being like everybody else. They focus on being exceptional. They stop doing what they aren't good at, and invest in growing their brilliance. They focus on becoming a master, and then they begin to innovate and develop new game-changing approaches. Because they are that good.

From the moment Jessica uncovered her true brilliance she became excited about her future. "This changes everything. I'd been planning on taking a course in analyzing stocks, but procrastinated about registering. Now I understand why. I don't want to become a master at stock advising. If I focused on being a guiding light in the retirement investment industry, I'd take a completely different path. And when I envision myself as a 'master' at this, I see myself speaking widely, maybe writing books, kind of like Suze Orman. Wow. I'm getting fired up now! I've already got an idea about the talk I want to put together that I could take to all the women's groups in the area. I bet that after a few talks, if I really listened to women's questions, I'd have the start of a really interesting e-book.

✎ YOUR TURN—Invest in Your Brilliance and Become a Master

What could investing in your brilliance mean to you? What would a path of mastery for your brilliance look like?

_____

_____

_____

Who exemplifies being a master in your craft? Who inspires you in your industry with their unique, highly valuable approach?

_____

_____

If you let yourself think like a master, who could you be in your field? What would you do differently that might even change the game in your profession?

_____

_____

After you've given some thought to investing in your brilliance and becoming a master, take a few minutes to jot down your development plan. What will you start doing? What will you stop doing?

1) _____

2) _____

3) _____

Jessica's plan included:

Join Toastmasters and grow my skills and confidence with speaking.

Develop a workshop for midlife women on taking charge of their financial wellbeing for life.

Take a class on writing for information products.

Stop trying to be a fast-trade financial advisor. Maybe look for a partner who likes analyzing stocks.

Your Passion Is the Compass

Over the rest of this book, your passion will provide the compass settings for all aspects of your business. When you structure your business, your passion will guide your decisions about what you do, and what you must delegate and let go of. When you design your marketing strategies your passion will make the difference between succeeding or fizzling, because when you're doing what you love it's much more likely you'll actually take action. When you share about your services, your passion will be infectious and attract the clients you can best serve. When you make your passion the centerpiece of your business, you'll stay energized, avoid burnout and keep your spark alive. When you design your business in harmony with your core, you put yourself in charge of your destiny and on a path of attracting on-going opportunities, making the money you want, and enjoying soul-level fulfillment.

Before we begin to design your business vision however, we have something important to do first. We are going to envision your life vision. This might sound odd, but for your business to serve your life, you'll first need to get very clear about how you want that life to look.

You are hard-wired from birth to be great at something. This is your unique passion, and you're meant to use it. Your number one job as a business owner is to discover your passion, and organize your business so you are using it most of the time. Passion isn't a luxury in tough economic times. It's your greatest asset. When you don't orient around your natural ability, you put yourself and your business at risk. When you know and trust your passion you tap into your true power. There are simple, but profoundly effective ways to pinpoint your passion. When you name and claim your passion, it immediately starts changing your life, business and path. Unleashing the full power of your passion takes investing in it and becoming a master. Your passion provides the underlying compass setting for all aspects of your business and will put you in charge of your destiny.

WHAT KIND OF LIFE DO I WANT TO AUTHOR?

What Kind of Life Do
I Want to Author?

"Tell me, what is it you plan to do
with your one wild and precious life?"
—Mary Oliver

For years I've felt irked when I read business planning books. They just didn't seem to start where I was in my life. They seemed to be missing something. At first I thought it was just me, but in fact, they've left out a crucial step.

Traditional business planning starts with the business. But for our business to serve our life, we first need to have a life vision.

As a creative woman entrepreneur, you already know how vitally important it is to have a clear vision in your business. In these times of unprecedented change and relentless turmoil, it's even more essential. When we have a guiding vision we're the creative force directing our business, no matter what circumstances, challenges or changes arise. We can live each day with an unshakable intention directing our actions, no matter what happens.

But even though you understand the power of vision in your business, I bet it feels much harder to do this for yourself and your life. The unending demands of our lives can distract us from asking the hard questions about what really matters, until we get a jolt of stark reality.

I became poignantly aware of this recently. Carol, my next door neighbour, a beautiful woman and mother of two, recently died of brain cancer. When I heard about her passing, I was in the midst of my annual visioning and business planning. The news shocked me, and for the next few days, I became very aware of the preciousness of life. When I looked into my husband's eyes, I lingered with a quiet appreciation for the moment. When I met a dear friend for a walk, I felt a rush of emotion rise in my throat. When I called my sister for our regular Saturday morning chat, I was unusually speechless for a few moments. All week, each client meeting felt sacred, and like an event to be savoured.

Carol's passing had jarred me awake from the usual rushed and pressured pace of life that often distracts us from our true selves. Out of that sad event, I gained some valuable insight about the pressing need to follow our dreams....today.

In this chapter you're going to make space for—and give audience to—your precious life dream. You are the CEO of your life and one of your most important jobs is to define your life vision. Not a picture that's a practical, predictable continuation of your life thus far. Rather, a vision that is based on what really matters. One that, if you lived it, would be an extraordinary life for you.

Dreams come in infinite shapes and sizes and are unique to each of us. One of my greatest joys is listening to people connect with their deepest desires. Sara's dream is to create a home-based business that allows her the time and flexibility for her special needs son while caring for her elderly mother. Deanne, a recent divorcee whose youngest child just left home, dreams of having a fulfilling career that expresses her buried inner artist and of finding true love at midlife. Lin Ho, an accomplished educator in Singapore and mother of two young girls, dreams of never returning to a 60-hour work week and of finding new home-based ways of generating income that allow her to use her gifts and be with her girls. Shelley yearns to become debt-free and build a highly profitable business that leaves her time to enjoy semi-retirement with her husband.

As you read the next few pages, take time to start thinking about your life vision. I challenge you to reawaken to your deepest desires and use them to envision the life you most want to live.

Why Do We Need Visioning?

Women especially seem to need visioning. When a woman comes to me for coaching she often has a very specific reason—"I'm here because I want more clients," or "I'm so busy I feel buried and don't know how to get out," or "I just can't seem to get free of my backlog and get on with growing my business." Sometimes, she can't really say why she feels stuck and confused. Either way—whether the focus seems clear or not—I know we need to start with visioning.

Visioning is actually a way to discover our deepest desires. However, this can be challenging. We often have many layers of wants, some of which we're unaware of. We might think we want one outcome, when we really want something else. We have a tendency to discount our dreams as unrealistic before we can even put them out into words. We often don't allow ourselves to dream big enough. We listen to all the reasons we can't do whatever our hearts and minds tell us we really want. We limit ourselves before we start and don't even realize we're doing it. We get tangled up in the "shoulds" and expectations of others and unwittingly cut ourselves off from our truth.

The goal of visioning is to move you toward your deeper desires. It is a way to reveal the true nature of what you love. It allows you to dream the really big dreams—the kind you assumed were impossible.

This can be scary. We're often afraid to admit to our deepest desires. Honestly embracing a dream means risking failure. What if we allow ourselves to really want something and it doesn't happen? That kind of disappointment is almost inconceivable. We've all learned along the way to defend ourselves from that level of vulnerability. Fear—the fear of failing, or being thought the fool, of being judged and rejected—makes us want to keep the dream buried. We learn to want less, make do with what we have, and be a little smaller. But when we do, we end up leading smaller lives. It takes a particular kind of courage to boldly listen to your quiet inner voice of knowing. When you do, it's the starting point of living a life you truly love. Tracey's story exemplifies the dramatic impact of this.

Tracey, an accomplished internet business pioneer at midlife, was struggling to define her business vision. We explored her passion and quickly laid out three potential business concepts, but she just couldn't get passionate about any of them. I sensed we were playing cat and mouse with a deeper truth, so I asked: "Tracey, what is it that you'd most regret not having accomplished at the end of your life?" There was a long silence, and then she whispered, "If I don't have a family, I'll feel that I've failed in what my life is about. I know it's outrageous at my age, but I just can't ignore this urge." Her deepest truth was out in the light. Though it had taken enormous bravery to reveal this to herself, we both knew she'd made the first important step in defining her extraordinary future. It took daring and determination to begin taking action, however as she did doors opened immediately. Within a few months she found an avenue for adopting a child abroad and she knew what her highest life vision was. Not surprisingly, her business vision seemed to take care of itself. Opportunities to earn money using her brilliance as an e-marketing consultant started flowing in. Though the road was one of the most demanding she'd ever walked, her personal strength, fulfillment and happiness soared to a new high.

With a little introspection, Tracey found the freedom to discover what was really important. Now I want you to give yourself that kind of limitless permission, to discover what you really want in your life. Over the next few pages, I'll share a step-by-step process to help you tap into your inspired life vision.

YOUR TURN—The Starting Point for Visioning

Does the idea of tapping into your life vision sound daunting? If so, I want to reassure you that it's easier than you think. When I work with clients, I'm amazed to see how our vision is right there, under the surface, waiting to be tapped. Our heart's vision isn't something we manufacture. It's already alive and present, waiting to be put into words. Let's start right now. Take five minutes to do a simple activity that is the first step in developing your life vision: take stock of what you love in your life now.

There is tremendous power in noticing what you value in your life, just the way it is right now. We move at such a rapid pace, we rarely stop to appreciate what we love. What's working well. What we cherish. When you stop to notice what brings you pleasure—the most alive parts of your life—you'll move naturally to your heart, the seat of your vision. Claiming what you love will help you know unmistakably what belongs at the center of your life vision.

Take out your VisionPlan notebook, turn to a fresh page and write, "The things I love about my life are…" and just start completing the sentence. Write down at least twenty points and feel free to write many more.

The things I love about my life are…..

_____

_____

_____

_____

_____

_____

_____

"We become what we love. Whatever you are giving your time and attention to day after day, this is the kind of person you will eventually become. Is this what you want?"
—Wayne Muller

Continue reflecting on this throughout your week. As you go through your life notice what you give your best attention to. Examine where you spend your favourite time. Look at your appointment book and your daily schedule. Notice the people and things that get your attention and love. Whenever you discover an activity, person, habit or aspect of your life that you love, jot it down on this list. A little later on, you'll be drawing on these as ingredients of your life vision.

The Power of Vision

Before we go further with visioning, there's one thing I want to sort out. A vision is not a fantasy. When you are living in a fantasy—hoping, wishing and wanting—it is actually an escape. It diverts you from a path of action that can actually lead you to a life you love.

A true vision is based in reality. It gives you an internal compass that directs your daily actions and behaviours. It puts you in the driver's seat of your life and ensures you are driving toward more joy, happiness and fulfillment. It generates an energy that infuses and lights up your present. You are empowered to move forward, make real changes and have the courage to act purposefully, whatever unpredictable challenges come your way. Let me give you a personal example.

A few years ago my Dad, who was 91 years old at the time, relocated from Florida to my local area. My sister and I had encouraged him for years to consider moving. When he made the decision, I was both excited about the opportunity to be part of his life on a weekly basis, and daunted by the radical change this would make in my business and life. How could I include a new, major priority in an already overflowing life?

Whatever doubts I felt, I knew my vision of an extraordinary life was to have a business that serves my life priorities. Being available to support my Dad was unquestionably living my purpose. After sharing my concerns and fears with my trusted personal advisors, I boldly declared a new possibility, a new extraordinary future—I would clear one day a week to be available to my father and my business would be more successful. Though it seemed outrageous to my logical self, a deeper part of me knew it was completely doable.

Over the next year, step by step, situation by situation by situation, this unbelievable vision came true. I enjoyed memorable days with my father and my work went to another level of richness and impact with revenues increasing by 15 per cent in 15 per cent less time.

When we courageously listen to our deepest commitments and walk our soul's path, unpredictable, fulfilling and seemingly miraculous results occur.

✎ YOUR TURN—Impact of Vision

When have you ever experienced the power of a bold vision? Take a moment to recall a time when you dared to pursue a possibility that seemed difficult, or illogical, yet you knew in your bones it was what you were meant to do.

What was the impact? How did it empower you? What did you learn about yourself and the power of vision?

_____

_____

_____

_____

_____

_____

_____

_____

_____

_____

_____

_____

★ COACHING TIP—VISIONING GUIDELINES

To get the most out of visioning activities in this book, I suggest a few guidelines:

- Carve out a time and space in which you can be totally focused on your visioning without any distractions.
- Go to one of your favourite soul-nurturing places. Somewhere you feel comfortable, relaxed and will have the privacy to claim this time just for you. It might be your bedroom, or a coffee shop, the library or a quiet place in nature. You might even want to book a weekend retreat at a local Bed & Breakfast.
- Choose a place that helps you shift out of the day-to-day press of life into the deeper currents of your soul.
- Create an inspiring environment. You might want to put on uplifting music, or light a candle, or position your chair so that you have a view of beauty.
- You can either do one exercise a day over a period of a few days or do all of them in a single session.
- None of these activities should take more than 30 minutes to an hour to complete. Be cautious about over-thinking or trying to make it perfect. Your visioning does not have to be perfect. Simply write down the answers that pop into your head.
- Recognize you might feel uncomfortable or embarrassed or resistant for all the reasons we've discussed. Remember, this isn't self-centred or self-indulgent. It's your job as CEO of your life and your business to define an authentic, inspiring and energizing vision.
- Visioning will quite likely stir your critical voice. You might want to take a moment to talk to the inner naysayer and ask her to take a break for a while. (You might even want to skip ahead to page 232, Break Through Your Inner Glass Ceiling if the voice just won't step aside.)

What Happens If We Don't Lead with Our Life Vision?

When we don't take the time to define our life vision, we risk the most common syndrome business owners face. We find ourselves crazy busy but ultimately unfulfilled.

Let's face it. Running a small business is a lot of work. Each day we wear many hats—serving our clients, marketing to attract new business, keeping track of our costs and revenue, and dreaming up the next new innovation.

Without first developing a clear life vision, our business vision can overwhelm the rest of our life. In extreme cases we may even cross the line from chronic overwork to workaholism. If we have only one thing in our life we do well and that one thing is work, we inevitably have our whole identity tied up in our work. We work longer and longer hours, gradually become isolated from friends, spend less time with our loved ones, neglect our self-care and eventually become disconnected from what matters most. We feel increasingly tired, guilty, stressed and even burned out. While we are a success at work, we forget or ignore what it means to be successful in our life.

When I started coaching Shelley, an Executive Coach and Trainer, she was on the brink of workaholism. When I asked her to tell me about her personal vision, she was confused. "My personal vision? What does that have to do with my business? Now that my children are grown, and about to leave home, I have so much open time that my business is my primary focus. I really don't think I need to spend time on my personal vision."

Immediately a red flag went up for me. Without a personal vision of a life worth going home to, I was concerned that Shelley was at risk of burning out. I sensed that her expectations of fulfillment through work just weren't achievable, because the most important element wasn't being addressed. Without a vision for her life, any work we did on her business vision could tip her over the edge. To work on her business we needed to start by unlocking what mattered in her life.

How to Tap Into Your Vision

Whether you feel crystal clear about where you are headed, or confused, stuck and disheartened, there are two simple yet powerful questions that will help you unlock your vision without fail:

What do you want?
What don't you want?

These questions are catalysts that will help you sift through your thoughts and discover your deepest intentions for your life. When you start exactly where you are, and ask yourself "What do I really want?" and "What don't I want?" your imagination will give words to your true heart's desires.

Even if what surfaces first is a string of statements about what you don't want in your future, it's good. Just write them down, stating them as clearly and specifically as you can. Part of the magic of using these two simple yet profound questions is that we always know what we don't want. (Even when a client is stuck-up-to-her-knees-in-mud stuck, she has always been able to tell me what she doesn't want!) Declaring what you don't want can be a powerful way to draw the line in the sand about complaints you no longer want persisting in your life. You send a clear message to the universe that you do not want this as part of your future. And knowing unequivocally what you don't want can point you directly to your real desires.

When I asked Shelley these two questions—What do you want? What don't you want?—she became quiet for a moment, and then said, "Well, I don't want Bill and me to drift apart. I can feel some distance in our relationship that wasn't there a couple of years ago. It seems whenever I get busier, he gets quieter. I wouldn't want my business growth to harm our marriage. And I don't want my health to decline. That series of colds I had last year and couldn't shake disturbed me. Another thing is, I don't want to feel so stressed that life stops feeling fun. That's why I started this business in the first place." She had begun to tap into her most important heart's desires.

After you've done this, step back, take a deep breath and read over your Do Want List. Does it feel delicious? Does it make you smile? When we let up what we truly want, it's as energizing as breathing pure oxygen.

When you've finished, put down your list and walk around. Take a break. Let your mind wander. Go for a walk. Allow yourself all of the work you've done to settle, and refresh yourself before we look at the key that will ensure the vision you're designing will in fact lead to happiness and fulfillment.

 YOUR TURN -- *What Kind of Life Do You Want to Author?*

Take a few minutes to relax yourself by stretching, doing some Yoga or just staring out the window. Take a few deep relaxing breaths. Go to your heart and signal to your inner wise self that you are ready to hear what's next for you. Start to think about the kind of life you want to author. Imagine it is some time in the future, perhaps two or three years from now, and things are going very well for you.

Now, turn to a fresh page in your VisionPlan notebook and draw a vertical line down the middle of the page. Title the left-hand column "What I do want is…" and the right-hand column "What I don't want is…" Just write what comes to mind as if you were emptying a cup.

What I do want is….   What I don't want is…

_____   _____

_____   _____

_____   _____

Shelley's list looked like this:

What I do want is….	What I don't want is…
• A thriving business	• For Bill and me to drift apart
• An abundance of work I love doing	• For my health to decline
• Make great money - $100K+	• To feel so stressed that life isn't fun
• To enjoy my life	• To work 60+ hours/week, 7 days a week. No break
	• Feel isolated, no social life
	• No time for "me," fun, family, my husband
	• Think about work obsessively

Don't second guess yourself, or over-think. And please don't let the very practical side of yourself start asking "How?" There will be a time for that, but it's not now. Allow yourself to dream. Think big. What does living an extraordinary life mean to you? Jot down ideas about what you do and don't want. Consider all aspects of your life. Here are a few suggestions to get you going:

- your romantic relationship
- your family
- your friends
- your home
- your work
- your creative pursuits
- your hobbies, travel, and fun activities
- your health and well-being
- your spiritual life
- our community and service activities
- your finances to fund this life

Next, let's take this a step further. Read through each "Don't want…" and dig deeper into what it's saying to you. If you don't want this, what do you want? Write the answer on your "Do Want…" list.

Finally, as an unmistakable, symbolic act indicating that this will not be part of your future, strike a line through the "Don't Want…" statements. Shelley's statements looked like this once she dug deeper, and turned them around:

What I do want is….

- A thriving business
- An abundance of work I love doing
- Make great money - $100K+
- To enjoy my life
- Clear boundaries between work and Personal time.
- Personal time.
- Able to shift gears. Present to my life.
- Stop working when I stop work, including mentally.
- One weekend day (at least) free of work
- Re-claim my passions of music & art
- Spend time with Bill. Quality 15 mins/day and a date night weekends.
- Self-care a priority.

What I don't want is…

~~For Bill and me to drift apart~~

~~For my health to decline~~

~~Feel so stressed that life isn't fun~~

~~To work 60+ hours/week,~~

~~To work 7 days a week. No break~~

~~To work continuously. No time for "me," fun, family, my husband~~

After you've done this, step back, take a deep breath and read over your Do Want List. Does it feel delicious? Does it make you smile? When we let up what we truly want, it's as energizing as breathing pure oxygen.

When you've finished, put down your list and walk around. Take a break. Let your mind wander. Go for a walk. Allow yourself all of the work you've done to settle, and refresh yourself before we look at the key that will ensure the vision you're designing will in fact lead to happiness and fulfillment.

Your Values, the Soul of Your Vision

What words speak of your personal values system,
what you stand for, what you want to live up to,
what you consider most important to your inner
life and wellbeing? —Robin Fischer Roffer

Shelley came to our next meeting with a nagging question on her mind. "How do I know my Do Want List is really my vision, not just a passing fantasy?"

I could relate. I too had doubted and second guessed my ideas about my vision for years. After I'd stated my heart's desires, I'd feel a gnawing unease and wondered if it was really what I wanted or just a daydream. Visioning often felt like throwing darts at a target in the dark.

The turning point came when I learned about the power of values. Our values are who we are at our core. They reflect our deepest commitments and the essence of what's most important to us in our life. When we base our vision on our true values, we know for sure that what we're envisioning will lead to happiness and fulfilment.

What matters most to you? What are your core values?

If just hearing these questions makes you break out in a sweat, you aren't alone. Usually when I first ask a client what their values are, they look stunned. It's a big question. Perhaps *the* big question in life. It's almost impossible to answer point blank, and rest assured, I won't be asking you to answer it cold. We'll be walking through a step-by-step process that will reveal your values effortlessly.

Define Your Values

Identifying your values can be the most powerful thing you do to live an authentic life. When I defined my values, I felt a deep sense of peace. What I stood for, unequivocally, was now clear. My life felt integrated. I felt anchored in my life purpose, and I had a clear understanding of how to direct my precious life energy each day.

When I work with clients to identify their values, they often tell me it cuts through competing demands and reconnects them in a deep and meaningful way. Life becomes simpler. They see where they should (and shouldn't) spend their time. They have a decision-making filter for their vision.

 YOUR TURN —*Define Your Values*

If you've worked through the activities so far, you've already laid the groundwork for identifying your values effortlessly. We'll take this in a couple of steps: first you will identify a few possible values, and then you'll focus them into your four core values. By the end you'll have a clear sense of your deepest commitments.

Start by rereading your Sweetest Moments (on page 29), Name and Claim Your Essence (on page 33), "What I Love" (page 45), and your Do Want List (on page 53). As you do the next activity, keep in mind your insights from these exercises. They hold many rich clues about your essential values.

Following is a list of words to spark ideas about your values. As you look over the list, I want you to circle any word that resonates with you. Pay special attention to those words that seem to jump off the page. Don't think too much about this, and beware of the tendency to choose words you think you should want. What we're looking for are the ones that genuinely light you up.

Abundance	Congruent	Orchestrate	Support
Accomplish	Connection	Originality	Synthesize
Adventure	Contentment	Patient	Taste
Alert	Control	Peaceful	Tenderness
Alter	Courage	Perceive	The Unknown
Arouse	Danger	Perfect	Thoughtful
Articulate	Dare	Persevere	Thrill
Artistic	Dedication	Persuade	To catalyze
Assemble	Delight	Plan	To contribute
Assist	Dependable	Playful	To create
Attain	Design	Pleasure	To discover
Attentive	Detect	Prepare	To experience
Attract	Devotion	Prevail	To feel
Augment	Direct	Provide	To feel good
Awe	Discern	Quest	To glow
Be accepting	Distinguish	Radiance	To lead
Be amused	Drama	Realize	To nurture
Be awake	Educate	Refine	To relate
Be aware	Elegance	Reign	To teach
Be bonded	Emote	Relate to God	To unite
Be connected	Emphasize	Religious	Touch
Be integrated	Encourage	Respond	Transform
Be joyful	Endeavour	Responsible	Triumph
Be linked	Endow	Risk	Trustworthy
Be passionate	Energize	Romance	Truth
Be present	Energy	Rule	Turn
Be sensitive	Inquisitive	Satisfied	Uncover
Be spiritual	Inspire	See	Understand
Be with	Instruct	Seek	Unique
Beauty	Integrate	Sensation	Uplift
Bliss	Integrity	Sense	Unstick others
Bravery	Invent	Sensual	Venture
Build	Laugh	Serenity	Vulnerable
Calm	Learn	Serve	
Capable	Love	Set standards	_____
Cause	Magnificence	Sincere	
Coach	Mastery	Space	_____
Comfort	Minister	Spark	
Community	Model	Speculate	_____
Compassionate	Move forward	Spirit	
Complete	Observe	Spontaneous	_____
Conceive	Open-minded	Stimulate	
		Strengthen	_____

This list of words is simply a brainstorming tool. Feel free to add any additional words or phrases that you feel are important that aren't on this list.

Now that you've chosen the words that attract you, I'd like you to pull out your top ten values. One way to do this is to put a check mark next to each word that feels really important.

For example, Shelley's top ten values are: Empower; Connect; Creativity; Adventure; Teach; Be awake; Create; Spirituality; Inspire; Love.

My top values are:

_____

_____

_____

_____

_____

Now you are going to focus even more. Of these 10 words, which are the most important to you? Identify the top four or five words that capture what is essential to you in life. Without them, life just wouldn't be worth living. Rather than thinking of excluding some of the words, you may find it makes more sense to look at how the words group together into clusters. Then, identify one word in each cluster that encompasses the others.

As Shelley considered each value, she saw they naturally grouped together as:

Love, empower, connect

Create, creativity

Spirituality, be awake

Adventure

Inspire, teach

> Look over your values and focus them into your four or five core values here:
>
> _____
>
> _____
>
> _____
>
> _____
>
> _____

Take a deep breath. Well done. Read over your list. How does it make you feel when you entertain these as your values? Delighted? Inspired? How do you think would it feel to live a life that fully expressed these values?

Some clients say they experience a deep relaxation and sense of rightness in their body. Others say they feel some shyness, or vulnerability. Seeing what matters, connecting with the core of who we are, means facing our magnificence. Seeing this can be awe-inspiring, but, as I said earlier, we've been trained to minimize our greatness. It makes sense that you might feel a bit embarrassed about your values.

I invite you to fully embrace them. Sit with them. Walk around with them for a few days. Let them settle in. Feel free to go back and refine or revise them in any way. These are your values. You will know when you have pinpointed your deepest commitments. Next, we'll pull everything together in your life vision.

Your Inspiring Life Vision Statement

If you've worked through these visioning activities you're most likely feeling an exciting, new possibility take shape. Next we'll capture all your clarity and inspiration in a concise, inspiring Vision Statement.

Okay, you might be saying to yourself that you don't really need to do this. After the many ideas you've jotted down, your vision probably feels so alive that it's almost palpable. Creating a written statement feels unnecessary.

But there's a funny thing about vision. When it's clear, it's crystal clear. And, then it's not! Have you ever had this happen? One day you're on fire with your vision and you're unstoppable. The next morning you wake up and it's vaporized like mist in the morning sun. We need a tool to keep the possibilities alive and help us connect with it even on the days when it's faded or disappeared. Crafting a Vision Statement will give you this tool.

We'll start first with a brief visualization, imagining that you're living your vision in full, vivid detail. Then we'll craft a simple, inspiring statement.

YOUR TURN – Envisioning Your Extraordinary Future

Allow about twenty minutes for this visioning process and ideally do it at a time of day when your energy is strongest. I suggest you start by reading over the insights you've jotted down in this chapter – What you love about your life, your Do Want list and your Core Values. Read through the following instructions to give you a sense of where we're heading.

When you're ready, sit in a comfortable position and allow yourself to relax. Stretch, take a few deep breaths, or do whatever helps you shift gears and bring your full attention to yourself and this moment. Close your eyes and bring your attention to your heart. Feel yourself sitting in the chair, and feel your breathing rising and falling. Let each breath relax you more and more and allow yourself to drink in the stillness and quiet of this preset moment.

Now, imagine you are in the future, two or three years from now. Things have gone very well for you. You are living a life that expresses your passion fully and freely. Your heart's sweetest desires have started to happen for you. You are being who you're hard-wired to be, every day. You are feeling happy and deeply fulfilled. Imagine that it's the morning and as you awaken, you look around the room and appreciate your surroundings. What do you see?

In your imagination, walk through your day. What are you doing? Who are you doing it with? What is your work life like? How is your health? What's the pace of your life? What are you doing that's fun? How are each of your values being expressed?

For the next few minutes, imagine what's happening in vivid detail. When you're ready, bring yourself back into the room by feeling your feet on the floor, and stretching a little.

Now, turn to a new page in your VisionPlan notebook, and take a deep breath. Recall the guided visualization, and the most important themes. Start writing your vision statement as if you're living it right now with a brief paragraph on each of those themes.

Here is Shelley's vision as an example:

MY LIFE VISION

I can honestly say I love my life. I know my soul values and life priorities and I honour them daily. I have clear boundaries between work time and personal time. I am fully engaged when I'm working, but never rushed. I feel present, and live at a pace that allows me to enjoy my life.

My days include time for "me" and time for Bill. I practice energizing self-care consistently. I take an hour each morning for to meditate, read, write in my journal, do yoga or walk in nature. Each day I have something to look forward to that makes me happy, like playing the piano, taking singing lessons or gardening. I am physically fit, feeling vitally alive and connected to my spiritual source. Bill and I spend some time together each day talking, sharing a meal or exercising. We have one evening on the weekend together no matter how busy our work lives are.

I value my friends and get together with them a couple of times a month. Bill and I socialize and entertain once a month and have developed a wonderful circle of couples we enjoy. I am delighted that I have flexibility in my work schedule that lets me 'hang out' with my son and daughter when they call or visit. I am involved in their lives as much as they want.

I am grateful for all the success I enjoy and make time to give back to my community. I always have a volunteer project on the go, helping young women or other causes that touch my heart.

Bill and I take two vacations a year, travelling and having adventures. We are aligned in our vision for retirement, and are on-track to being finan-cially independent in 10 years. As well, we experiment with RV travel to see if we want to do this in the next chapter of our lives.

Each day I live with gratitude to Spirit for my healthy, loving relation-ships, fulfilling work and many blessings.

MY LIFE VISION

✭ COACHING TIP

Here are a few tips to make your Vision Statement as energizing and alive as possible:

Write is as if you already have it. State it in the present tense, using vivid emotional language.

Avoid using words like "should" "ought" "will" "perhaps.": When we use these words we are probably in our head (not our heart). These words are clues that this isn't our authentic vision, but someone else's. When we try to live out someone else's dream, there's no juice in it. It won't give us the power to achieve it, and even if we did accomplish it, we wouldn't feel fulfilled.

State it in positive terms. Avoid stating the negative: "I won't be as stressed" is still focused on stress. Instead, state it positively like "I am calm, present and fully engaged in the moment."

Make sure your vision describes both the desired (external) conditions for your life – what you have, what you are doing and who you are doing it with – and the (internal) experience of who you are being and how you feel. You'll unlock the transforming power of vision when it evokes your feelings. Imagine having what you want and doing what you want. How would you be feeling? What difference will this make? What will you have that you don't have now? Capture the essence of your vision vividly.

After you've written a paragraph for each important element in a very specific way, describing it in as much detail as possible, read each paragraph out loud to yourself. How does it sound? Is it what you really want? Is it authentic? The truth will be in your voice. Does your voice sound unsure or flat? If so, there might be an inner critic at work. Think again about your "wants" (not your "shoulds"), and rewrite it. Do you feel excitement while you're writing and reading? Great! It means you're getting to your passionate vision and tapping into the energy you'll need to live your dream.

Don't be afraid to rewrite or refine your vision statement. I want you to shape this until it feels right for you and makes your heart sing. Soon, the energy of your vision will infuse your life, and have a focusing effect in your daily activities.

Congratulations! You've taken an important step that many business owners overlook. You have a clear, guiding vision of the life you want to author. You've given time and attention to your precious life dream. You've defined what living an extraordinary life means to you. Now, let's design the blueprint for the business that will take you to this future.

For your business to serve your life priorities, you need to have a vision for your life. Visioning is a way to discover your deepest desires. Embracing your vision can be scary because you risk failure. When you give yourself permission to discover what's really important you unleash the power to make real changes. A vision is not a fantasy. It's based in reality and leads to meaningful change. When you don't lead with your life vision you run the risk of having your business overpower your life. Defining your life vision is easier than you think. It is right beneath the surface waiting to be uncovered. You can uncover your vision by noticing what you love, listening to what you want and don't want, understanding your values and imagining your most desired future. A written vision statement helps keep the essence of your vision alive even during difficult challenges. Your vision of an extraordinary future puts you in the driver's seat, driving toward joy, happiness and fulfilment.

WHAT DO I REALLY WANT FOR MY BUSINESS?

What Do I Really Want for My Business?

*"Most people determine what is possible by looking
at history, industry orthodoxy and immediate circumstances.
Start with looking at your soul and gaps in the marketplace
at the same time and dare to conjure up an impossible dream.
Ask, What if...." —Robert Hargrove*

Now that you have a picture of the life you want to live, it's time to design the business that's going to help you realize it. It's time to craft your Business Vision. Your Business Vision is a clear statement of the business you want to build, that will ultimately make your life dream possible.

What do you *really* want your business to achieve?

If you can't answer immediately, you're not alone. We often walk around with vague, general ideas about our business dream, but end up focusing only on this month's problems. We talk about wanting something different, but get lost in the demands of the next email. When we're unclear about our Business Vision, we feel a gnawing undercurrent that something is missing, but we can't put our finger on what it is, let alone start doing something about it.

Kristin, a successful Personal Trainer and Life Coach put it this way: "I'm feeling kind of flat today. There's nothing really wrong, I just don't feel motivated." As we explored further, she said "I was really successful last year – best year yet – but I just feel 'done' with doing my business that way. I don't know what the next dream is."

I've heard clients say it many ways:

"This economic downturn has affected my clients. My best profit centre has dried up and I don't know where to go next."

"I'm just generally feeling frustrated, like something is aching to happen, but I don't know what it is."

"I'm actually on-fire with possibilities for my business but I feel like I'm running in all directions at once. I don't know where to start."

However we state it, the issue is the same: feeling at a crossroads without a roadmap forward. What's needed is an authentic, passionate, inspiring Business Vision. You may think you don't have one, but don't worry. Even if you can't state it right now, your Business Vision (just as you discovered with your Life Vision) is right beneath the surface waiting to be put into words.

That's what this chapter is all about.

Why Do We Need a Business Vision?

When we don't take time to develop a clear vision, we leave the direction of our business to moods, whims, fears and the demands of others. Without a guiding vision we feel unfocused, unsure of what to do *now*, pulled in endless directions and at risk of burning out from scattering our energies. We simply can't access the deep wellspring of commitment, motivation and energy that the daily tasks of growing a business require. Decision-making can be scary and difficult. Unless we have a Business Vision, we'll second guess ourselves every step of the way, and fail to use our best qualities to move forward.

When we do the work to tap into our inspiring vision, it not only gives us a clear goal to steer toward, it has another even more important impact. A compelling vision generates a palpable energy field that has an immediate positive effect. It will permeate all aspects of your business and influence everyone who touches it – you the owner, your staff, your clients, and your potential clients. You become empowered to move forward. Your clarity and passion will attract clients and give them an enlivening experience that will make them want to let others know about you and your services.

You know this experience. Think about your favourite store for a moment, and recall the last time you visited it. Quite likely just thinking about this experience is making you smile. The Body Shop, the personal care products store founded by Anita Roddick, is an inspiring example of this for me. I love the Body Shop products and have been a loyal customer for years. Her game-changing vision revolutionized the cosmetic industry in the 70s when she launched her first store. She broke the mould for how women's cosmetic products were merchandized by eliminating expensive packaging, and offering excellent products at affordable prices. Over the decades her vision as a social entrepreneur set new trends by advocating fair trade products, championing important causes while continuing to offer highest-quality products and personalized, friendly customer service. Just walking into one of the stores lifts my sights higher as a business woman and challenges my assumptions about what my business could bring to the world. When you become clear about *your* compelling Business Vision, it will have a similar enlivening and attractive impact on your business, customers and industry.

Over the next few pages I'll share how developing a compelling vision transformed Kristin and her business. Though she'd just achieved her best year yet as a personal trainer, she felt flat, restless and trapped. As she tapped into her true passion and took risks to express it in new ways, she unleashed a contagious enthusiasm that infused her work with new joy and drew people to her new services.

Tap Into Your Business Vision

Now, I want to be clear about something. Business Vision isn't just enthusiastic talk and pie in the sky dreaming. It involves listening intently to your quiet inner voice, seeing real needs in the marketplace, and inventing new (even game-changing) ways to fulfil them – then passionately and wholeheartedly committing to these possibilities and making them a reality.

Your Business Vision starts with your imagination. It is a bold declaration of what you most want to have your business become. Just like you discovered with your Life Vision, a compelling Business Vision isn't something you can figure out by looking to your past and trying to predict a guaranteed future. It isn't a managerial projection; you don't take what you did last year and extend it a little. Similarly, you can't find it by looking to others for the solution. You unlock your vision of an extraordinary future for your business by asking the big questions like, "What do I *really* want?" "What difference do I want so passionately to make that I'd be willing to re-invent not only my business but myself?"

Okay, probably just the mention of those questions is causing your stomach to make a turn or two. If the idea of creating a Business Vision seems daunting, I want to reassure you that, just the way with did when we crafted your Life Vision, we'll take this step-by-step.

🖎 YOUR TURN —The Starting Point for Your Business Vision

Let's take 10 minutes and dive in right now. Just as you did when you launched into visioning about your life, we are beginning by looking at what you love about your business the way it is today. You've already felt the impact of claiming what you love in your life. It's similar with your business. Appreciating what you love about your business naturally moves you to your heart, the gateway to your Business Vision. Claiming what you love will help you know for sure what belongs at the core of your business dream.

Take out your VisionPlanning notebook and turn to a new page. Write "What I love about my business is..." Start by thinking about your business now. What do you love about it? What brings you pleasure, enjoyment and a glow of satisfaction? Just start completing the sentence. Write down at least twenty things you love, and I challenge you to write many more. If you get stuck, think of a satisfying day you've had recently in your business. Mentally go through each detail that made you happy and write it down.

When Kristin looked at what she loved about her business, her list looked like this:

- love working in fitness, helping people with their physical fitness and wellbeing
- answering questions about nutrition and fitness routines
- being well-known, respected where I work
- feeling confident, kind of an expert in what I do
- love talking to people about their big dreams and goals
- love learning about new techniques, like the Pilates Reformer

What I love about my business now is…

_____

_____

_____

_____

_____

_____

_____

_____

Complaints and Gripes

Perhaps as you looked at what you love about your business, another voice started chattering away too: "But, I don't like (x, y and, z…)." Now, give that voice room to speak. Turn to a new page, and write "What I can't stand about my business is…."

A good dose of negativity can been good for your soul. Good, enthusiastic complaining not only lets off some steam, but will immediately point to the aspects of your business you've outgrown. You have full permission to call a spade a spade, complain, and kvetch about what's not the way you want it.

What's most upsetting? Irritating? Downright unpleasant about your business now? Be specific. Don't let yourself slide by with generalizations like, "I work too hard." Write instead "I just can't stand that I work 50 to 60 hours a week. The point of self-employment was freedom not slavery!" Make a thorough list. This will not only release pent up energy, it will give you valuable clues about your emerging Business Vision.

When Kristin just let herself vent honestly, her list looked like this:

- I hate having to get up at 4:30 am and being at work by 6:00 am 5 days a week
- feel bored with the same thing over and over again
- politics at the club. Just feels too hard to not step on egos every day
- frustrated and I don't know why
- feel constricted
- hate the paperwork
- can't stand being measured by quotas.
- feels like the club is my whole "world." Too small.
- I'm over 45 years old now, and my body just isn't the same. The work is 100% physical. How long can I keep this up?

What I can't stand about my business is….

_____

_____

_____

_____

_____

_____

_____

Just keep completing the sentence until you've emptied the cup. You will know when it's time to stop. Now, stand back, take a breath and read through everything you've written. If anything else springs to mind, just jot it down. We'll be using all of these later to envision a business you will truly love.

The Business Vision Formula

A successful Business Vision has many facets and there's a formula that helps captures this in a simple way:

Passionate Services + Ideal Clients   + Optimal Business Vehicle

= Business Vision

Over the next few pages, we'll use this formula to shape your Business Vision. First, you'll envision your passionate services (What do you want to be *doing?* What services do you most want to offer? Who will these services allow you to *be?*) Next we'll envision your ideal client (Who do you most want to serve? What are you doing for them? What needs are you resolving for them?). Then we'll design a business structure that allows you to do your best work, profit financially and live the lifestyle you truly desire.

Finally, we'll pull all the elements of your Business Vision together into an inspiring, focused statement of precisely what you are building.

Now, just one note. Tapping into your Business Vision isn't a linear process. Feel free to read through the next three chapters and move among the facets in the way that makes sense to you. Each element relates to the others. Insights about one will feed and fuel the others. Trust yourself as we work through these questions. Remember to tune into your intuition. These questions are simply prompts. Trust that you *know* on some level exactly what you want next in your business. Turn off your inner censor when you do these activities. Allow yourself to explore, be playful and have fun. This is *your* business. This is *your* vision. You get to do this *your* way. And, as you move forward, you get to change it as your vision evolves.

Let's get started by looking at the first facet of your Business Vision, your passionate services.

Your Passionate Services

*"A business absolutely devoted to service
will have only one worry about profits.
They will be embarrassingly large."*
—Henry Ford

Imagine you could do exactly what you want to do in your business.
What would you be doing? What services would you offer?

Your passion is the starting point in defining your services, because
if your heart isn't in the work, if it isn't meaningful to you, you simply
won't have the energy and whole-hearted commitment required to be
successful. You won't invest the time it will take to grow a successful
business. You won't have the spark to stand out from similar professionals and be attractive to your potential clients. When your services
are based on your passion you'll enjoy your business so much that your
work will feel like play.

You've already done the hard work of pinpointing your passion and
your essence in Chapter 1. Now we want to envision the business services
that will leverage them and make a unique and needed contribution to
others.

When I asked Kristin, the personal trainer, to envision herself doing
what she does best 80 per cent of the time, she was silent. Even though

she was considered a leader in her profession, she'd been feeling bored for quite a while. "You know, that's an interesting question. I'm doing what I do well, but there's no challenge in it any more. I feel like I'm walking through the motions with my clients."

"What's not quite right, Kristin?" I asked. "It just feels too small," she replied. "I don't want to just run people through their routines. I want to touch them more. I want to do deeper work. I still want to work with people's bodies, but I want to address their minds and souls too. I love it when the light bulb comes on for people and they make a major change in their health and well-being. I want more of *that*. You know, I've felt for a long time that I want to work with groups. Now I'm beginning to see why."

I asked Kristin to explain. Immediately she said, "Well, I'd get to be The Adventurer. That's my essence. When I'm being my authentic self, I'm The Adventurer, and I love to challenge people to climb *their* Mount Kilimanjaro. If I were fully being my real self in my business, I'd be doing *this* most of the time." With this insight, she had started re-inventing her services and her entire way of running her business.

 YOUR TURN – *Your Passionate Services*

What do *you* want to be doing in your business? What are *your* ideal services? To answer these questions, we'll start first by taking stock of your current services and then we'll pinpoint the emerging, new directions.

Part I: Turn to a fresh page in your VisionPlanning notebook and draw three columns. Title the left-hand column "Services Now," the middle column "What I love/enjoy" and the right-hand column "Complains/What I want to be free of".

Start by jotting down your current services, and then recall working with your clients this past month. As you remember your best moments as well as your frustrations, sort through what you most enjoyed as well as your complaints. Kristin's list looked like this:

Services Now	What I Love/Enjoy	Complaints
1-1 training in the gym	• I'm masterful. Know what I'm doing • Talk about tips • Motivating while training • "Light bulb" moments • Get motivated and make big changes	Kind of boring Just physical exercise Feel frustrated. Want to do so much more.
Small groups about fitness	• Get to work with more people • Enjoy being in front of the room • Fun performing • Can go into more depth	
1-1 client in home gym	• "My space" • Design. customized to each person • Can go deeper	

Services Now	What I Love/Enjoy	Complaints/Want to be free of
....	....	....
....	....	....

✑ *Part II: What new services do you want to create?*

Now, let's turn to the inklings and urges about the new services you'd love to develop. What wild and wonderful ideas do you daydream about? If money weren't an issue, what would be the most fun to do? If you knew you wouldn't fail, what new service would you launch? Then go even further. Dig a little deeper and ask, "What appeals to me about this? What will this allow me to express that I can't now in my business?"

When Kristin considered these questions her worksheet looked like this:

One new service I want to create is:

- A workshop that lets me touch people more in-depth

  What appeals to me about this?
- Get to be *me*...The Adventurer
- Get to use my depth of experience as a former elite athlete. Self-mastery
- Motivation. Share all my learnings about working mind, heart, soul and body

One new service I want to create is...

_____

_____

_____

What about this appeals to me? How would it express my passion?

_____

_____

_____

_____

Next, we will consider who you most want to serve in your business.

Your Ideal Client

"Your most perfect customers are patiently waiting for you. In fact, they are looking for you and are counting on you to [shine your light] so that they can find you at the most perfect time and place."—Stacy Hall & Jan Brogniez

Who is your ideal client? What is their greatest need? How do you want to serve them?

If you are like most of my clients when I first ask them these questions, you might be thinking right now, "Well, how should I know?" I've asked hundreds of talented, self-employed professionals, from seasoned veterans to initiates and their immediate responses range from silence to confusion to shocked disbelief. The notion that we can set our sights on attracting an ideal client, let alone create a business completely filled with them might seem audacious, unrealistic and impractical—especially now in times of market turmoil. Shouldn't we be glad to take whatever we can get? Isn't this a time when we ought not be too picky and just do our best to work with whomever comes along?

In a word, no.

You and your business have been created for a specific purpose and to serve a particular group of clients in a particular way. One of the key facets of your Business Vision is to understand who you're meant to serve and how. I'm going to help you identify characteristics of the individuals or organizations that make them absolutely ideal for you to work with.

When I started my business, my first inclination was to work with anyone who showed any interest in my services (even if they couldn't pay me!) Then my business mentor coach asked me to describe my ideal client. The question stopped me in my tracks. How would I know? Did I deserve to work with only ideal clients? The question rocked my thinking. You see, for the past six years, in my work as an in-house career coach, I had been required to work with anyone and everyone who came to the programs I offered. I'd become a master of accommodating, adapting and twisting myself out of shape to "make it work" with my clients. The notion of choosing my clients, and only working with people who were ideal seemed unbelievable. Thank goodness I found the courage and took this approach to heart. It has become an unfailing guide to my true work and to the people I'm meant to serve. It has increased my joy, headed off significant problems, caused leaps in my productivity, kept me focused and on my purpose line. It has helped me build an authentic, attractive brand that has brought me more clients and referrals than I can handle.

Is it possible to create a profitable business that consists completely of clients who are attracted to doing business with you?

In a word, yes.

Not only is it possible, it is the most direct path to a financially stable and prosperous business and soul-satisfying work. You see by doing this, you'll also be sharpening your "entrepreneurial vision." You will identify *your* ideal clients, learn what their real needs are, and innovate the services and products that you, and only you, can uniquely provide. It is the formula for an endless flow of work, financial rewards and success through serving.

What is an Ideal Client?

An ideal client is one whose needs are a perfect fit for your company's mission. When the relationship between need and service are aligned amazing results occur.

Pause for a moment and picture your ideal client. When I ask women business owners to do this for the first time, they often say they don't know what is ideal for them. But they always know what *isn't* ideal. Your inner compass is continually giving you clues. Once you pinpoint what is *not* a fit for you, you can develop a clear profile of what would be an optimal fit by identifying the opposite.

Marie, the personal chef, had a shockingly clear experience of the difference. "Last week I was invited to interview for being the personal chef to a well-known celebrity in the city. At first I was elated. It sounded like a dream opportunity. The man who was recovering from a significant health issue, wanted a personal chef to cook healthy, gourmet meals according to his doctor's guidelines. This is one of my specialties and I was excited. However, fifteen minutes into the interview, the dream felt more like a living nightmare. I just wanted to get out as fast as I could." Later, as she mulled over what had happened, she realized he was angry about having to give up his long-time pleasures of rich food, wine and cigars. To him the personal chef, no matter how talented, would be an unwelcome agent of an unwanted change. "He was as far from my ideal client as they come."

By contrast, a few days later Marie went for an initial consultation with a young executive in the financial services industry. "I couldn't believe the difference", she said. Even though he too had recently been told by his doctor to follow an extremely restricted diet in an attempt to lower his cholesterol, each suggestion she made delighted him. "When he hired me at the end of the interview, I felt like I'd fulfilled my deepest desire for my work. I was helping someone make the life-enhancing changes in their eating they truly wanted to make."

We always have a choice about who we bring into our business. Each of us decides who and what is a great match for us. What is ideal for you won't necessarily be ideal for the next person. You are the only one who knows what is a perfect fit for you.

But how do we recognize our ideal clients?

There is a kind of chemistry, almost a magic, in the connection with an ideal client. You've probably felt this many times. Take a moment to think of one of your favourite clients. Remember what it was like when you first met, and the way you feel when you work with him or her.

We recognize an ideal client the moment we meet one. There is an immediate spark of attraction. There's a feeling of mutual respect and admiration. As we hear about their situation and challenge, there's a quiet knowing that we can make a significant contribution to resolving their problem and enhancing their life. Almost instantly we're sharing information and resources freely. We sense our passions and values are similar. Quite likely the client draws out our best work and we feel fulfilled. It's almost as if we've known each other for a long time.

Conversely, when we work with a client who is not intended for us, the mismatch becomes apparent instantly. The interaction is difficult, confusing and taxing. We feel frustrated, tense and anxious. They want us to provide a service we do not normally offer, or want us to make an exception to our policies, or change our pricing. We leave the conversation feeling emotionally drained and less certain about the value of our services.

As you choose to work only with people who inspire and energize you, you will truly enjoy the work you're doing, do your best work, which in turn makes you more attractive to other potential clients.

 YOUR TURN—Envision Your Ideal Client

While you may have thought about these questions before, I invite you to engage them with a fresh mind. We are going to get them out of your head and onto paper where they can start to focus your intention and shape your Business Vision. We will look at three questions: Who is your Ideal Client? What is their greatest need? How can you help them resolve it?

Who is your Ideal Client?

Rather than making a list of qualities for your ideal client, we're going to start with a brief visioning process.

Begin by pulling out your client list. If you don't have one at your fingertips, take a few minutes to put together a list of the clients you've worked with over the years. Once you have it in front of you, read over the list try to recall your experience with each client. Who did you enjoy working with?

Who truly valued working with you? Which clients felt more like play than work? Make a check mark beside your favourites. Next, narrow this list down to the best of the best until you've identified your top three to five most delightful and fulfilling clients.

Now, shift gears and get ready for a brief visualization. Sit in a comfortable chair with your feet flat on the floor. Uncross your arms and legs and take a few gentle relaxing breaths. Allow each exhalation to release tension and relax your mind.

In your mind's eye, imagine yourself in a safe, nurturing environment. Imagine an inviting, creative workspace. It might be your actual office, or an imaginary place that feels comfortable and is just right for you today. When you feel comfortable and relaxed, invite in your favourite clients. Imagine all of them come in, and sit across from you. They are really pleased to be here and are eager to support you in growing your business. They have come ready to be interviewed by you.

Look at the first person and think back over your relationship with them. What attracted you to this person when you first met? Bring to mind your working interactions. What did you most enjoy about serving this person? What qualities and characteristics made your work together positive? Now consider, what had them seek out your services? What was their greatest frustration? What emerged as their compelling need?

Next, reflect on the work you did together. What did you provide, from their perspective, that made the difference?

Give yourself sufficient time to think about this person, what you enjoyed about serving them, their true needs and how you contributed most.

When you feel ready, move on to the next person. Consider the same questions. What did you enjoy most about working with this person? What characteristics made the relationships so positive and successful? What was their greatest issue? How did you make a substantive difference to them, from their point of view?

Continue with the visualization until you have conversed with each one. Take all the time you want and when you feel you have finished, thank them and imagine them leaving.

When you're ready, take a few gentle, deep breaths and come back into the room. Turn to a fresh page in your VisionPlanning notebook and write down what you learned from this visualization.

Client Name   **Characteristics I most enjoyed**

_____   _____
_____   _____
                                                            _____
_____   _____
_____   _____
                                                            _____
_____   _____
_____   _____

Need from client's perspective   **What I brought that
                                                            they appreciated most**

_____   _____
_____   _____
_____   _____

_____   _____
_____   _____
_____   _____

Ideal Client Profile

Next, we'll pull these insights together into a simple snapshot of who you want your business to serve. Turn to a new page and title it "My Ideal Client." Review what you've just written, and pull out the positive qualities, characteristics and attributes you identified in your most favourite clients. Feel free to add any qualities or traits that would make it a delight to work with a client, even if they aren't on your list from the visualization.

Characteristics of My Ideal Client

_____

_____

_____

_____

_____

_____

_____

_____

_____

When you feel the list is complete, put your pen down and take a deep breath. Read over your list, tweak or add to it until you feel you've captured what's important.

Next, we are going to distil this into the top seven characteristics that define your ideal client. We want to transform this from a laundry list into a focused intention. Feel free to combine points and prioritize the traits until the profile feels right to you. Here are what Kristin's and Marie's final ideal client profiles look like.

Ideal Client Profile:
Kristin, Personal Trainer, Workshop Leader and Coach

- Health conscious. Wants to improve their fitness or lose weight. Has a big goal.
- Mid-life woman
- Open to, or passionate about inner work (personal growth)
- Already has a fitness routine and exercises. Wants more.
- Successful. Can easily afford my fees.
- Ready to make changes and take action.
- Well-connected. Will refer spontaneously when they like my services.

Ideal Client Profile:
Marie, Personal Chef

- Busy professional, executive or business owner
- Loves great food. Values health. Nutrition conscious. Possibly special dietary requirements.
- Within a 30 minute drive of my home.
- Easy to load in and out of their home, i.e. few stairs.
- Want service regularly, like every 3 weeks or more frequently.
- Good kitchen. Well-equipped. Everything works.
- Can easily afford my fees (e.g. saving money by not ordering in).
- Well-connected in their community and refer my services.

My Ideal Client Profile

1) _____
2) _____
3) _____
4) _____
5) _____
6) _____
7) _____

As you read over your profile, does it make you smile? What if your business was filled with clients like this?

In a future chapter we'll look at the most effective ways for you to find these ideal clients. For now, post this description in a place where you can see it every day. Just focusing your intention on who you most want to serve sets in motion a series of changes that help you connect with the people you are meant to serve. As you read over this profile, ideas will probably spring to mind about how you need to up your game to appeal to them. Kristin immediately saw that she needed to get out into her community and be more visible to mid-life women, and joined a local business networking group. Marie realized she wasn't mentioning she specialized in health issues and changed her 10-second introduction to share her passion for helping busy professionals who need to change the way they eat.

Let's turn to the third aspect of your business vision, designing the structure for your business that will allow you to do your best work, serve your clients well, and enjoy the life you want to live.

Your Optimal
Business Vehicle

*You are a product of your environment. So choose
the environment that will best develop you toward your
objective. Are the things around you helping you
toward success, or are they holding you back?*
—W. Clement Stone

Imagine it is a couple of years from now. You've had a great day. You pause for a moment to take a breath and just let it all in. You have arrived. You are living your dream. Things have gone very well and you have created your business *your* way. You have designed and built a business that is ideal for you. It brings out your best work, leaves your clients feeling well served and very satisfied, and it supports a rich and rewarding life for you.

How does this business look and feel? What shape has it taken?

In working with hundreds of women business owners, I've had the opportunity to see the unlimited ways we can design our businesses. Shelley, an empire-builder, wonders how big she can go with her executive coaching business. Marie, the Personal Chef and former corporate refugee wants a home-based business that gives her freedom, variety and full creative expression. Deanne, a motivational speaker wants to travel the world through her work.

As you work through this section, you might discover that overall you are very happy with how your business is set up and you just need to make a few tweaks. Or you may discover that you want to completely re-think and re-invent your way of structuring your business. I'd like you to consider these questions with curiosity and an open mind. Give yourself full permission to admit what you really want. Remember, your vision about your extraordinary future is just beneath the surface waiting to be seen.

Here are several questions to help you design the ideal structure for your business:

What's the optimal size of your business?

Is your dream to create a large organization? Or is a boutique practice most ideal? How big do you want your company to become?

What revenue do you want to generate?

Is this a large, full-time business, generating a six- or possibly even a seven- figure income? Or is a part time practice that compliments your other life priorities ideal? We'll go into more depth about your revenue plans in a future chapter, so at this point just state a revenue target that captures the type of business you really want.

What is the geographic scope of your business?

Do you want to serve your immediate community? Or have a regional, national or global scope?

Who do you want to work with?

Ideally, do you want to work alone as a solo-preneur? Or would working with a partner or a team of colleagues lead to greater success and fulfilment?

What hours do you want to work?

How many hours do you want to work each day? Each week? How many free days do you want?

What type of organization do you want to build?

Do you want a company with employees? Or a single assistant? Or would you prefer a "virtual team" of subcontractors?

What amount of travel would be ideal?

Do you want to travel for business? Where? How much would be optimal? How much would be too much?

Kristin's worksheet looked like this:

Optimal size/type of organization: I want to be based in a club half of the time and in my home gym the other half. I want a boutique practice to start. Perhaps I'll grow it larger after that, but I want to have a solid, profitable practice, be fully in charge of my schedule and work life before I consider growing it larger. I want to become really well-respected for my unique blend of physical training and coaching in the areas of weight loss, nutrition, and midlife health.

Revenue: I want to generate about $75,000 this year with the potential of growing to $100K in the next two years.

Geographic scope: I want to focus on my local community, within a 45 minute drive of my home gym.

Work alone or with others: I want to work as a solo-preneur primarily. I'm interested in exploring some alliances on projects in a year or two once I've built my new brand.

Hours: I want to work no more than 40 hours a week. I'm fine to have a couple of clients on Saturday, if I have half a day of personal time midweek. I want to stop working at 3:30 pm four days a week. One day a week I'll take clients in the evening.

Staff/Support: I don't think I need any employees or support staff now. Maybe a virtual assistant to help me with administrative work once the groups take off.

Travel: Minimal commute. I want to stop in-house private training sessions as soon as possible. I want my private clients to come to my home gym. I want to commute no more than 10 minutes to the club. In a year or two my wildly wonderful dream is to have one adventure trip a year, either for professional development like a conference, or for an adventure tour with clients.

YOUR TURN – Your Ideal Way to Structure Your Business

Start by turning to pages 71 and 72, and read over "What I Love Now, and What I Just Can't Stand." If any new ideas have come to mind, add them. Then, take a deep breath. Let your imagination shift to the future about two to three years from now. Imagine you are doing your business exactly the way you want to do it. It's bringing out your best. It fully supports you in giving extraordinary service to your clients. You are inspired when you walk into your workspace. You have the tools and equipment you need at your fingertips. Your systems bring an increasing sense of ease. You have fun delivering your services. Take a few minutes to imagine this future with as much detail as possible.

If the niggling question, "But how is this going to happen?" surfaces just detach from it for now. We'll get to that question a little later on. Right now, it's completely fine if you don't know how this will become a reality. Simply imagine the most enjoyable, fun, exciting and effective way of doing your business.

When you are ready, open your VisionPlanning notebook to a fresh page, and start writing down what you want. Here are the questions again to prompt your ideas:

How are you doing your business? Home-based? Environment outside your home?

_____

What size is your business? Large? Boutique? Part time? Full time?

_____

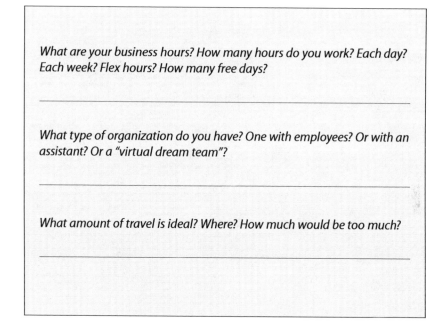

What are your business hours? How many hours do you work? Each day? Each week? Flex hours? How many free days?

_____

What type of organization do you have? One with employees? Or with an assistant? Or a "virtual dream team"?

_____

What amount of travel is ideal? Where? How much would be too much?

_____

If you've mapped out the activities in this section, you've now defined all the elements of your authentic, passionate, inspiring Business Vision. Well done! You've designed your passionate services. You've envisioned your ideal client. You've outlined your optimal business vehicle.

Next, we'll pull all of this together in an inspiring Business Vision statement.

Your Business Vision Statement

"The future is not something we're going to,
but one we are creating." —John Schaar

Our final step will be to pull all your insights together into a simple, inspiring statement. It will describe the clear future direction you're steering toward, and it will serve as an inspiring reference to ensure you are always reminded of what you're doing and why. It will inspire you to live your dream and help keep you on-track, focused and motivated.

 YOUR TURN—Pulling it all Together

Start by reading through all your notes from the exercises in this section. Now, take a deep breath and imagine it's a couple of years in the future. Things have gone very well. You are singing your song. Your business is thriving. What's happening?

Take a few minutes to envision your extraordinary future.

Close your eyes, take a few deep relaxing breaths and bring your attention to your heart. Imagine yourself walking through a typical day. You are doing what you love doing, and fully expressing your unique, passionate essence every day. Your business is filled with wonderful clients who seek out and are grateful for your services. Your business is structured in a way that is a joy to do, and just keeps getting better and better. You are confident and thriving in your work. You feel challenged creatively are a master at your craft and feel more and more fulfilled daily. Let yourself drink in the richness of your extraordinary future.

When you're ready, shift your awareness back into the present. Turn to a fresh page in your VisionPlan workbook and again take a few deep, refreshing breaths. Recall your visualization and start writing your vision statement. Just as you did with your Life Vision, use the present tense and vivid, evocative language. Write what you are doing, experiencing and enjoying as if you are living it now.

For example, Kristin's business vision looked like this:

I am excited to be creating and living my ideal business Transformational Fitness Inc. I am a dynamic, well-known personal trainer, workshop leader and coach. I'm one of the leading authorities in the Boston area on midlife fitness and wellbeing for women. I've developed a signature program that inspires, informs and coaches people in succeeding in making big health changes.

I have the ideal mix of services: I work part-time in a well-known fitness club, and part-time in my home gym. I offer one-to-one private fitness training sessions, small group training and workshop. My true passion is leading the Breakthrough Program which is my unique approach. I share my top tips from being an elite athlete and I'm known for my "depth" approach.

I enjoy working with my most ideal clients who are midlifers, especially women who are health conscious, value fitness, have big goals and are ready to make changes. I seem to naturally attract people who understand that the "inside-out" approach is what leads to permanent, life-long change.

TFI generates $75,000 per year and I work about 40 hours a week. I have enough flexibility in my schedule to enjoy the freedom of self-employment. My business is a success and I'm thriving because I get to be "The Adventurer" in everything I do.

MY BUSINESS VISION

Craft your Business Vision here. Allow your imagination total free play. Keep it as specific and concrete as possible, pulling together your most important desires and key points.

_____

_____

_____

_____

_____

_____

_____

_____

_____

_____

_____

_____

_____

_____

_____

_____

_____

_____

_____

_____

_____

Once you have written your vision statement, describing your desired future, stand back and take a deep breath. Read it out loud. How does it sound? Is it what you really want? Is it authentic? As you did with your Life Vision, check your voice. Does your voice sound unsure, or flat? If so, give yourself complete permission to reconsider it. Think again about your wants, and re-write any parts that don't feel quite right. Do you feel excitement while you're writing and reading? Great! It means you're getting to your passionate vision and tapping into the energy you'll need to create this.

Now, there is just one final step to take. Boil this down to one sentence that captures the essentials of your vision into a succinct snapshot.

✍ YOUR TURN—*My Business Vision Snapshot*

Use this simple template to distil your business vision into an inspiring, affirmative statement of no more than 30 words. By limiting the amount of words you use, you'll zero in on what really matters, and have a memorable snapshot of the future you're creating.

I, _____ , am growing _____ into a
      Your name   *company name*

successful _____ in _____
      type or description of business   *geographic location*

generating _____ providing _____
      revenue   *descriptions of services*

to _____ within the next ___ years.
    description of your ideal customers/clients

Kristin's snapshot looked like this:

I, Kristin Jones, am growing Transformational Fitness Inc into a successful fitness and wellbeing company within the Boston area generating $100,000 revenue providing individual training, workshops and coaching to women within the next two years.

Don't be afraid to refine or completely re-write your vision statement. I want you to shape this until it feels right for you and gets your creative juices flowing. You'll know when you've got it: the energy of your vision will fuel you, and positively impact all who touch your business.

Well done! You now have a clear statement of the business you want to build that will support making your life dream possible. You are no longer walking around with vague, general ideas about your business dream. You have a clear future direction you're steering toward. I imagine you're feeling a kind of calm excitement when you think about what you're creating.

Next, we'll dive into the question that will tap into an inner force that will be key to this vision of your extraordinary future becoming a reality.

Your Business Vision is a clear statement of the business that will ultimately make your life dream possible. When you operate without a vision, your business is directed by your whims, fears and the demands of others. Your Business Vision is right below the surface waiting to be put into words. Your vision isn't an extension of the past. It's a bold declaration of what you most want to build. Your vision gives you a clear future direction to steer toward, and it energizes your present. Your Business Vision has three facets: your ideal services, your ideal customer and your optimal business vehicle. Your best services leverage your passion and make your work will feel like play. You and your business have been created to serve a particular group of clients in a particular way. When you identify your ideal clients, understand their real needs and innovate solutions that serve them, you tap into an endless flow of work and rewards. Your ideal business vehicle allows you to do your best work, serve your clients and enjoy the life you want to live. Your simple, inspiring Business Vision statement gives you a reference to help you keep on-track, focused and motivated.

WHAT IS MY TRUE NORTH?

What Is My True North?

"It's not what you sell, it's what you stand for."
—Roy Spence

I've got a tough, but exhilarating question for you.

Why does your business exist?

I said it was a tough question. But, here's the thing. You are going to work many hours, invest an ocean of love, energy and innovative ideas in growing this dream. I want your efforts to give you the rewards your soul yearns for. The key lies in knowing and navigating by your True North.

Your True North is the compelling reason your business exists. It's your purpose. Your mission. The core, meaningful and inspiring difference you are trying to make in the world. Just like True North on a compass points the way, your business purpose is an inner force that will lead you to an extraordinary business.

Your business is unique because you are unique. There has never been one like this before in history and there will never be again. Your purpose captures this uniqueness in a simple statement that will guide all aspects of your business.

What Difference Does Purpose Make?

Purpose is the soul of your business. When you take the time to deeply understand and articulate it, the impact goes far beyond simply putting words on paper. You crystallize the important work of your business, ignite unstoppable motivation, establish a guiding beacon for your actions, and harness a powerful message that speaks directly to your ideal clients.

I first experienced the galvanizing impact of purpose when I was on the leadership team of a national non-profit organization. It was a few weeks after the founding partners of the organization resigned. The three of us who were now the leadership team, and suddenly responsible for the organization, were reeling with our new roles. The organization's bank account was nearly depleted and if we didn't grab the helm quickly, the doors would close in a matter of weeks. For hours we analyzed the situation, discerned the real needs, and brainstormed possibilities until the walls were covered with flip chart pages filled with ideas. Though a vision had emerged, we felt confused and lost without a sense of clear direction. Then someone asked, "So, why do we exist? What's our mission? If we did close the doors, what would the world be missing?" The simplicity and urgency of the questions cut through the fog like a sword. Within a few minutes we'd crystallized what we as a team were committed to bringing to the world. We felt lit up with an unstoppable passion. We knew that if we didn't do this, it wouldn't happen. We were on fire about our mission being accomplished. We'd found our True North.

While the idea of having a True North for your business may feel new, the experience is one you know instinctively. Think of all the organizations you've dealt with in your personal and professional life. You can immediately tell the difference between businesses that have a strong sense of purpose, and those that don't. In a business without a purpose, people may be busy but the effort feels frenetic, disorganized and directionless. When a business is purpose-led, everything makes sense and flows naturally. Let me give you a couple of examples.

Diane, a gifted healer and body worker, had dabbled in her practice for many years. When her son was leaving home, she sought out my services to help her grow her business. She enjoyed her healing work very much, but I noticed immediately that her level of engagement varied dramatically from week to week depending on her energy level, her moods and the demands of family members. She noticed this too and became curious about her sporadic follow through. As we explored her business mission she had a dawning awareness about what was going on. "I realize that something is missing. I don't actually have a sense of purpose for my business. Doing healing bodywork is more of a hobby. I love it, but it doesn't really matter if I do this business or not, even financially. I've always been financially supported by my husband, and compared to what he earns my income is pretty insignificant. I've never really thought that my work might matter, might make a difference." Without a heart-felt sense of purpose, she just hadn't been able to access the deep well-spring of courage, initiative, vision and staying power that come when we are planted in our mission.

Contrast this with Sara, a coach for people with ADD who was on fire with a sense of mission from my first conversation with her. "Sara, why are you growing this business? You have a rich and varied professional background and you could do anything you want to. Why this business now?" "Well," she said, "my number one priority is being available to my son, who has special needs. He is at a crucial age and having a home-based business is critical." She paused thoughtfully for a moment, and went on to say "Beyond that my husband and my son both benefited tremendously from working with an ADD coach. The research and tools literally saved my marriage, turned around my husband's career and put my son on a path of healthy social and academic development. I'm so passionate about making this information available to everyone who needs it that I literally jump out of bed every morning. I can hardly wait to get going!"

Starting from purpose is not idealistic. In fact, it's the *most* pragmatic way to approach your business. When you know your compelling "why" – both for yourself personally and for others – you tap into a power that will affect all aspects of your business.

- You have unstoppable motivation that will sustain you through any outer challenges.
- You have a transforming power that will dissolve all inner resistance.

- You have an inner compass that will guide your business through turbulent changes in economic conditions.
- You make decisions with less effort and greater confidence.
- You see more clearly what services and products will uniquely serve your clients.
- Your business has a purpose-led culture that will inspire those who work with you.
- The infectious energy of your business is highly attractive to potential clients.
- When you have a purpose-led business you will never be out of work. Even if you are temporarily without clients or projects, you can never be fired or laid off from your mission. There is always an abundance of work to be done to fulfil your unique business purpose. You will have endless opportunities where your gifts are needed to meet the real needs of the world.

With an authentic, enduring mission you access the determination, inspiration and drive it takes to turn your dream into a clear success.

 YOUR TURN—*True North Assessment*

Before we dive into defining your True North, you might find it useful to take a quick measure of where you are right now. Use this assessment to find what you can build on and what still needs to be discovered. Circle the number that reflects how you feel right now. One indicates a low level and five is high.

I know what I do best and love doing.	1 2 3 4 5
I've identified a real and meaningful need in the marketplace that my business can fulfil.	1 2 3 4 5
I know what my business doesn't and won't do.	1 2 3 4 5
I know the ultimate value my services/products make to my clients.	1 2 3 4 5

I can articulate the difference I'm passionately trying to make in my community/the world.	1 2 3 4 5
I communicate my purpose enthusiastically.	1 2 3 4 5
My clients, employees/subcontractors, referral partners, and stakeholders are fully aware of my business' purpose.	1 2 3 4 5

What did you discover from this? There are no right answers. This is simply a quick check-in to help you pinpoint the actions to focus on over the rest of the chapter. Where you scored a 4 or 5, the ingredients of your mission are probably quite clear. A 3 or less indicates there is more discovery to be done. Take your time and pay attention to what your insides are saying. Soon these will be clear too.

Women & Purpose: Do Women Play Too Small?

Last year, when I was a guest on a web radio program, I was asked a question that stopped me in my tracks. "Do you notice that women business owners tend to play too small?" the interviewer inquired.

As I considered the question, I realized that yes, there is some truth here. I had seen, both in myself and in the many women I'd coached on their higher business purpose, an almost apologetic holding back when we delved into our deepest desires to make a larger contribution. It is as if we need permission to care this much. Is it okay to think as big as we feel in our heart of hearts? Are we allowed to say we want to contribute something big and meaningful? I say that we are.

Our higher purpose is a declaration. Each of us has the ability to be audacious – to boldly state our highest vision and the role we will play in making it happen. There is a beautiful story of three stone cutters that captures the transforming power of living from a greater purpose. A visitor arriving in a village saw three stone cutters working in the heat of the mid-day sun. She walked up to the first stone cutter and asked, "What are you doing?" "Breaking rocks" he replied. The visitor moved to the second workman and asked again, "What are you doing?" "I'm feeding my family." The visitor turned to the third stone cutter and asked once again, "What are you doing?" "I'm building a cathedral," he replied with a sense of awe in his voice and a spark of the divine in his eyes. When you allow yourself to declare your highest aspirations of how you want to contribute, you are enlivened with the same spark as that inspired craftsman.

🖎 YOUR TURN—Permission to Play Your Biggest Game

Are you giving yourself permission to think big? To own your highest aspirations of how you want to contribute to an extraordinary future for others? Or are you keeping yourself small? Marianne Williamson stated it clearly, it is not our inadequacy we fear but our magnificence.

Imagine for a moment that it's a few years in the future, and you're being interviewed about your business. The reporter asks, "What motivates you? What is your highest aspiration for your business?

Is just thinking about this stirring some discomfort? Some fear of your magnificence? Or are you raring to go? Write down what comes to mind for you when you entertain playing your biggest game.

_____

_____

_____

_____

What if you gave yourself full permission to 'think big'?

Find True North

You don't need an MBA to craft your mission statement. This is not a complex process that requires advanced expertise. I want you to toss out anything you've heard about creating a purpose, or crafting a mission statement. We aren't going to spend weeks discussing and analyzing and debating this. I will show you a straightforward way to discover your True North and develop a simple, snappy statement that will inspire you and speak directly to the people you most want to serve. Your business purpose is natural. It already exists and is waiting to be put onto words.

I had a startling experience with this a couple of years ago. I was leading a day-long workshop with a group of 12 women who worked in early childhood education at the Annual General Assembly of the aboriginal bands in my local area. Throughout the morning I was moved by their concerns and touched by their aspirations for their communities. As we dove into the section on Mission, I wondered if it would make sense, or would it sound too "business-ese". A few minutes later I was stunned and inspired by the power of purpose. Eloise, a young woman in her early twenties, shared her larger vision and mission. "My vision is a safe community. I dream of our community being free of gang violence. My project is 'Safe Streets.' Our mission is to take back our community through empowering our youth." I was astonished by her clarity and the simplicity of her mission.

Defining your business mission is not a complicated, intellectual process. For us passion business owners it is written in our hearts, just waiting to be put into words.

3 Questions to Help You Find Your True North

I want to share a simple approach to uncovering your business mission that I learned about ten years ago from Thomas Leonard the founder of Coach University and one of my most important coach mentors. He used three simple, yet profoundly evocative questions to help people connect with their most inspiring business mission.

What do you want for others?

What do they need to have that?

What is your role in making that happen?

Let me share a conversation demonstrating the impact these questions had for Julie, a highly accomplished coach and consultant. We were just finishing the first draft of her VisionPlan, when we hit a wall.

"I don't know," she said. "I've defined my dream for where I want to take my business next—a $300K coaching, training and membership community for women business owners – but something is missing. It feels flat. It feels like a lot of work. I'm feeling quite heavy and discouraged."

"Julie, why do you want to create this new expression of your business? What do you want for women business owners? What do you know is possible?"

"I feel a little embarrassed saying this. I'm not sure if this is what you're getting at. I want women to find their voice. I believe we are at a point in history where it's time for more of the divine feminine in the world. That's my highest aspiration."

"What will women need to bring more of the divine feminine into the world?"

Julie was quiet for a few moments. "Well, a couple of things. They will need support. Support in trusting themselves, trusting their inner knowing, and their intuitions. And they'll need practical tools and skills."

"As you consider your essential values and your gifts, what could you provide that would help women trust their knowing and be empowered to put it out into the world," I asked.

"I am passionate about teaching women technology and e-marketing. I believe if women harness the full potential of the internet for getting their message out into the world it could unleash a powerful force for good." Julie paused for a moment. "Wow! This is very inspiring to me! This helps me understand why I've been dreaming about building a $300K business. While the revenue is appealing, I now understand what it really represents. Just sharing this mission with you has ignited something in me. My whole business plan is feeling different."

Julie had linked her business to a larger vision, and engaged an energy, a force that would take her and her business where she is meant to go.

YOUR TURN —*Find Your True North*

Why does your business exist? Turn to a fresh page in your VisionPlanning notebook, set aside about an hour to reflect on your larger vision and business mission. To tap into your True North, your business purpose, you need to identify how you most want to improve the quality of life for others. Trust yourself to know. Be prepared: when you first delve into identifying how you most want to contribute, you might feel confused or intimidated. Simply trust that your business mission is already written in your heart and is waiting to be put into words. You will find it by listening to your intuition and trusting your inklings and urges. When considering the question, take your time and be specific.

QUESTION 1: What do you want for others?

Bring to mind your ideal clients, the people you most want to serve. What do you want for them? If you could give them a gift, what would you give them? If you could resolve or transform their most pressing issue, what would you resolve? If you could contribute to this community, what would you contribute? What do you believe is possible? If your business accomplishes its highest aspiration, what will the result be?

This is your higher vision. Dr. Martin Luther King said, "I have a dream…" This is your heart's dream for humanity. For Eloise, her higher vision is a safe, gang-free community. Sara wants anyone and everyone with ADD to stop struggling, know their strengths and thrive in their relationships and work. Julie wants women to find their voice and bring more of the divine feminine to the world.

Now, just to be clear, you don't need to know how this will happen. In fact, the nature of a higher vision is that it is beyond what we personally can accomplish. However, in our deepest knowing place, we sense this is possible. It is an evolutionary trend. It is a greater divine order that wants to be realized.

As you think of the people you most want to serve, let your highest vision emerge as you answer these questions:

What do you most want for others?

_____

_____

If you could give your ideal clients a gift what would you give them?

_____

_____

If you could resolve or transform their most pressing issue what would you resolve?

_____

_____

If you could contribute to this community, what would you contribute?

_____

_____

What do you believe is possible?

_____

_____

If your business accomplishes its highest aspiration, what will the result be?

_____

_____

QUESTION 2: What will they need to have that?

Imagine a future where your ideal clients are living this vision.

What did they need in order for this to happen?

Eloise knew that the youth need to have alternatives to gang life. They need a peer influence that believes in them, that stands by them. They need education about alcoholism and drug addiction. They need stories and role models about alcohol- and drug-free lifestyles.

Sara knew for ADD sufferers to experience a new level of success and confidence they need access to information, and emotional support as they make changes as well as stories about people who are accomplishing their dream and living *with* ADD.

Julie knew that women need support in trusting themselves, their abilities, and their intuition. And they would need practical tools and skills to communicate.

What will your ideal clients need to have this higher vision?

_____

_____

_____

_____

QUESTION 3: What role can your business play in making this happen?

From all the activities, services and products your business could provide, what will most directly contribute to this higher vision happening? What is the unique role *your business* can play? How will your business support filling this need?

Eloise sees that her project can provide esteem-building activities to the youth through participating in making change happen in her community. First her organization will recruit youth to the project and engage them in all aspects of a fundraising event from getting the word out, to performing, to preparing food. Then the counsellors will teach life skills including compassionate communication to build self confidence and demonstrate a different way of making their place in society.

Sara is enthusiastic about her company providing education on leading edge research and best practices for self-managing ADD. Her business will create tools and provide support to ADDers through teleclasses, webinars, educational products and individual telephone coaching.

Julie passionately wants her business to teach women about technology and e-marketing. She will do this through an online community membership website, tele-seminars, group coaching, educational products and individual coaching sessions.

What is your business's contribution to making the greater vision happen? What is the unique role *your business* can play? From all the activities, services and products your business could provide, what will most directly help fill this need?

Defining Your True North

Now we will put these ideas into a succinct statement that inspires and directs you. A successful mission statement is short, memorable and motivating. It evokes an emotional response. It describes why your company exists, both from your point of view and your clients'. There are many ways you can shape this, and no one right way. What matters is that it speaks to you, is easy to remember and communicates powerfully to the people you most want to serve. To get you started, we'll explore three different examples of ways to format a purpose statement:

True North for My Business

Turn to a new page, take a few deep breaths and start playing with the elements you discovered when you asked the three questions. Pull out the words that speak to you most. Play with one or all of these three formats until one clicks.

1. Snappy statement approach: One way to crystallize the essence of your True North in a simple statement using six to eight words. Daniel Pink describes this approach as "making mantra." Your statement is catchy, inspires you and speaks directly to the heart of the people you most want to serve. Eloise's mission looks like this:

"Hands-on opportunities for a hand-up."

2. Who + Benefit approach: This format is a two-part statement capturing who you service and how they benefit:

We help _____ (your ideal clients)
_____ (goal or benefit of your services)

Sara used this approach and states her True North as:

"We help ambitious ADDers harness their strengths and take charge of their lives."

3. How + Who + Impact approach: A third approach is to pull together the three key ingredients of into a compelling statement. What does your business do? Who does it serve? What is the ultimate value you provide?

_____   _____   _____
Verb   Who   Impact/Value

Julie expressed her True North this way:

"Empower women business owners to express their voice more fully through harnessing the power of the internet."

My True North

_____

_____

_____

_____

Give yourself the freedom to create a rough first draft. You can always rework your True North statement in any way you wish. Remember, this isn't about getting it 'right.' There is nothing rigid about this. You are creating a simple statement that inspires you and will speak to the heart of the people you want to serve. The value of this statement is in its usefulness to you and to your business. It will have value if it has use and meaning to you.

Once you've crafted your statement, here's a quick checklist to ensure it's truly your guiding purpose:

- When I say this, do I feel inspired?
- Does this provide a sense of direction to my business?
- Does this articulate the deeper reason my company exists, beyond making money?
- Will this speak to my ideal clients?

The real test is, does is feel right? Keep in mind that stating your True North is a process that takes time. It's completely fine to walk around with this, try it on for size and hone it until it harnesses your passionate commitment to the real difference you want your business to make.

If you've tackled this tough but vitally important question, well done! It takes daring and bravery to 'play big' and put your highest aspiration for your business into words. Defining your True North unleashes an inner force that will inspire you, guide you, give you unstoppable motivation and help you share your heart message with the people you're meant to serve. Now that you know your True North, let's move on to the next powerful question that will help make your dream a reality.

Your business mission is the soul of your business. It already exists and is waiting to be put into words. With an authentic mission you tap into a well-spring of motivation. A purpose-led business can thrive in any economic condition. You have permission to think big and contribute something meaningful. You find your business mission by listening to your intuition. Three questions that will help you unlock your vision are: What do you want for others? What will they need to have that? What is your business' role in making this happen? When you link your business to a larger vision you tap into a force that will take you where you are meant to go.

WHAT IS
SUCCESS NOW?

What Is
Success Now?

"A vision without a goal is simply a fantasy."
—*Debbie Ford*

You've accomplished a lot over the past few chapters. You've pinpointed your unique, passionate abilities. You've envisioned a life filled with meaning and purpose. You've pictured the big idea for your business, and aligned it with your True North, which will guide you as you build the business you love.

Now we're going to put legs under this vision. It's time to create a game plan that will turn your vision into your new reality. Over the next few chapters we will chart your course so that you'll know where you're going, how you'll get there, and when. We'll go through a simple yet powerful planning process that will define your top business goals for this year, design your core business-building strategies, and ignite new results using action projects.

A well-conceived plan turns on a power that can seem almost magical. Conversely, if we don't take the time to construct a well-laid out plan, it's like embarking on a journey with no map. We start out inspired and excited about our grand adventure, but without the direction of a plan, we're doomed to disappointment.

Investing time, energy and effort in planning—even when it feels boring, tough and daunting—is absolutely essential. It will save you stress, anxiety, detours and regrets later on. Even though it's quite likely your plan will change, having this framework in place will allow you to change course in response to challenges or opportunities with less anxiety and more grace. The first step in developing your game plan is to define your most important goals for this year.

Success Now

I can almost hear you saying, "I've got an inspiring vision. Isn't that enough? Why do I need to set goals when I have a vision to guide me?"

While your vision is essential, it's not enough of a roadmap on its own. You see, your vision represents what's possible. It's a beacon on the horizon that will light the way to your destination. It will inspire you, energize you and pull you forward. Your goals on the other hand are the milestones along the way as you live this vision. They map out the specific, concrete results you intend to achieve that will spell success. When we confuse vision with goals we feel overwhelmed, confused and frustrated and don't understand why.

Sara, the ADD coach to entrepreneurs from Chapter 4, came to our meeting bubbling with enthusiasm. Over the Christmas break, she'd spent many hours in conversation with her business partner, dreaming about where they wanted to go next. They'd filled flipchart pages with possibilities, and invented exciting new programs for their clients. As she shared the vision, she was electric with anticipation. Suddenly she became quiet, and her mood shifted. "You know," she confided, "It's kind of odd. We mapped all this out about a week ago. I felt so great because I know it's the right direction. But since then, I've felt immobilized. I actually feel overwhelmed and scattered. I'm inspired by all the possibilities but I don't know what to do with them."

This is the impact of having a vision without goals. We are on fire with possibility, but at the same time feel confused, even overwhelmed. We are excited, but immobilized. Without concrete goals we wander directionless and can only hope and wish that things start to happen.

If we don't ground our inspiration in goals, the energy of our vision quickly dissipates and fizzles out.

Goal-setting is the step that will give shape to your inspiration, focus your ideas and harness your creative power.

Why Don't We Set Goals?

Let's face it, setting business goals can be tough. Why is that? Part of us knows we're getting serious now. We're not just dreaming and visioning. We're focusing and committing. Things are getting real and that triggers resistance. It's important to address this before we start to craft your goals.

I imagine you know a lot about goal-setting. We hear about it relentlessly in business classes, self-help books, even magazines on grocery store news racks. All this knowledge should be helpful right now, but I bet it isn't. I've noticed a funny thing with many of my clients. They're goal-shy. Over the years, they've picked up a bad case of goal-itis. There are many versions of it that go something like this:

> *"I've set goals in the past, but when I don't reach them, I just feel bad about myself. I don't think I want to set them again."*

> *"When I set goals, I just start feeling driven and pressured. I don't want to feel stressed that way."*

> *"I've set goals, but it didn't make any difference. I still didn't get what I wanted. I don't know why I'd do it again."*

I know. I've been there. A few years ago I had a case of goal-itis so bad that I refused to set any goals. But, you know what? That wasn't the solution either. I felt directionless, like a high-powered sports car, revving its engine with nowhere to go. I became determined to find out what it takes to stop suffering and learn to use the power of goal-setting in a joyous and effective way. That's what the rest of this chapter will show you.

✒️ *YOUR TURN—What Stops You From Defining Your Goals?*

Do you suspect you have a little goal-itis going on? What stops you from translating your inspiring vision into goals? Check off any of these that resonate with you, and add your own form of goal resistance:

- When I don't reach my goals I just feel bad about myself.
- Goal-setting makes me feel driven and pressured. I don't want to feel stressed that way.
- I've set goals, but it didn't make any difference. I still didn't get what I wanted.

_____

_____

_____

_____

_____

_____

Now, take a deep breath. Let go of your experience of goal-setting in the past. We'll be doing it a little differently. Purpose-based goal-setting will help you sidestep these pitfalls and learn how to harness your creative power in a new way.

Why Does Goal-Setting Work?

We human beings are naturally goal-oriented. When we have something meaningful to look forward to, it brings out our best. Think back to when you were a kid. I have a hunch you set goals all the time. "Today, I'm going to ride my bike all by myself." "I bet I could sew a dress for my doll on my own." "I haven't climbed that hill yet. Tomorrow I will." Goal-setting was spontaneous, a form of play. We instinctively used it to challenge ourselves and unlock our potential.

In contrast, when our goals are vague or undefined our whole system slows down. We become sluggish, depressed or even physically ill. Brain research is now helping us understand what's happening.

We have, at the base of our brain stem, a built-in control centre called the Reticular Activating System that can help us achieve our goals in seemingly amazing ways. Moment by moment this group of cells, about the size of a little finger, sorts and evaluates incoming data. It determines, from the thousands of sensory messages bombarding us, which will get through to our awareness. It filters out unnecessary distractions. It attunes us to valuable information and resources that help will us accomplish what is important, wanted and valued by us.

You've probably experienced the eerily odd effect of your RAS at work many times. You decide on the make and model of the new car you're going to buy, and then suddenly you see it everywhere. You make a commitment to start a new activity but aren't sure quite how to begin, and a book literally falls off the shelf at the library. We've all had it happen.

You can harness this natural ability and put it to work in amazing ways. The key that activates the RAS is commitment. When you choose a goal, you're declaring a new significance. You are saying this is important to me, this matters. Doing this sends a powerful signal to your RAS, literally programming it to bring you information, resources and ideas, even ones you aren't aware exist. The more passionately committed you are to your goal, the clearer the message you send to your RAS.

Kristin, the personal trainer from Chapter 3, felt the power of choosing a goal. She came to our meeting on fire about launching the new 8-week program she'd been dreaming about for a while. She came to our meeting on fire about launching the new 8-week program she'd been dreaming about for a while. "I'm so excited! This will let me talk about weight loss, fitness and nutrition, and delve into the mental mindsets that help us make a permanent change. I can see everything I want to talk about, laid out week by week." She paused. "But to tell you the truth, I'm nervous. Will people get what I'm offering? I'm known for physical training. Will they understand it if I start talking about their attitudes? I guess it's the leap I'll just need to take." She took a deep breath, and committed to share her deeper message.

When she arrived for our next call she was almost breathless with enthusiasm. "You won't believe what happened! The day after we spoke, I talked to one of my clients about my ideas for the new program. She immediately understood what I was offering. It was unbelievable. The day before, Oprah launched a week-long series on making lasting health changes, and all her experts were saying it's an inside-out process! Everyone I've talked to saw her shows, and understood my approach. They are all signing up! They feel lucky to have their own local coach who can work with them with this inside-out approach." Okay, coincidence? Or the 'magic' that happens when we make a firm commitment to our goals?

Purpose-based Goal-Setting

The secret to highly effective goal-setting is to base our goals on our purpose. When we do, we combine the "spirit" of the goal with the "form." When we start with our purpose and vision, our goals become simply pointers along the way. If we're being who we are meant to be, if we're living our purpose, we can never fail. We might get side-tracked along the way, but when the goal is purpose-based we can quickly learn from our missteps, correct our course and get back on track. We are freed from feeling bad about ourselves when we miss a goal because it's all part of the learning. It's completely fine if the goal changes or evolves. We aren't trying to adhere to a pre-conceived picture; we're listening to the deeper guiding intention and continually realigning our focus to what is most important.

We're going to use purpose-based goal-setting to define your most important business goals in three steps. First, you'll start by discovering one over-arching theme that spells success for your business this year. Next you'll uncover the core success indicators of your business and define goals that reflect real progress in these areas. Finally, you'll engage the full power of purpose-based goal-setting by committing and detaching.

Your Over-arching Theme

What is most important in your business this year? What is it that, if accomplished, you'd know you succeeded?

When Sara, the ADD coach, first considered these questions, her brow furrowed. "I haven't been thinking about it this way. I've been focused on my vision, but I see now what you're saying. It will take me at least two, maybe three years to grow my business to that big dream." The fog was starting to clear: "When I imagine feeling truly successful a year from today, there are a few key things I'd want. I would have a full practice, I'd be earning my living fulltime through my coaching work, and I'd have a marketing engine bringing a steady flow of clients. That would be real success for me. I'm excited just thinking about it." Brainstorming these results was helping her see what's important, as well as what's not the priority for this year. "I see now it's just not possible to bring on-line all of the programs I've dreamed up, at least not right away. I'm feeling relief already."

We probed a little deeper. "Sara, we want to find the underlying theme that captures the spirit of what you're up to. Imagine you have everything you've just said. You've accomplished what's most important toward your dream and you're feeling deeply satisfied. What would this bring you that you don't currently have?

It took Sara a few minutes to crystallize what mattered most to her this year. "Right now, I'm still feeling kind of small. I'm only known by a limited circle of people in my local area." She paused for a moment, and then went on to say "My dream is to go very big with this, open up a global market, especially in the French-speaking world. But I know I won't do all that in the coming year. You know, I think I've got it. 'Boldly Out There.' That's my theme! If a year from now I am boldly out there, speaking, marketing worldwide and confident that I can carry this message, I'd know I'd been living on purpose and in a whole new place."

This simple phrase defined her overarching theme. She'd captured her underlying, guiding intention that spells success for her business this year.

 YOUR TURN — *Your Overarching Theme*

Start first by reading over your Business Vision statement (from pages 94 and 95) and your True North (page 112). Imagine you're living your purpose now and moving boldly toward your highest vision. Take a moment to experience it, enjoy it and feel it.

Now, imagine it's a year from now (if you've just started your business, or you're new to goal-setting, you might prefer to use a 6-month time frame). You've accomplished what's most important toward your dream and you feel deeply satisfied. You're in an entirely new place in your business and your sense of yourself. You've succeeded, and you feel quietly fulfilled.

What have you accomplished? What results have you achieved that made this significant difference?

Jot down ideas as they come to you. Just brainstorm quickly and write them down.

What I've accomplished a year from now:

_____

_____

_____

Now, read over all your ideas and ask yourself:

What's <u>most</u> important? What is it that, if accomplished, would be real progress?

_____

_____

_____

What will this bring me that I don't currently have?

_____

_____

_____

What's my over-arching theme for the year? Capture your insights in a simple, inspiring phrase or word.

_____

_____

> If you're finding this tough, don't worry. Trust your intuition to let you know what's most important for you this year. Take a break, walk around for a while or do whatever helps you relax as you continue to consider your overarching theme and just jot down the ideas that come to you.

Define Your Top Goals

Next you'll shape all the ideas you've just brainstormed into a few key goals—but not just any goals. We want to pinpoint the ones that will put your hands on the helm of your business and steer it masterfully toward success. This takes identifying the core success indicators of your business.

I first tapped into the power of core success indicators when leading the non-profit organization. We were at the darkest point of the transition I mentioned earlier in Chapter 4, only weeks away from running out of funds and having to close the doors. New to the leadership role, I was assaulted daily by a mountain of information, challenges and demands. I teetered on the brink of complete ineffectiveness when a new question occurred to me. "How will we measure success? When this turns around, when we are out of the morass and are viable again, how will we know?" As a team, we sifted through all the information, issues, desires, targets and wishes we'd brainstormed and boiled it all down to seven factors that, if achieved, would make everything work out. We set up a tracking sheet and every Monday morning I was briefed on where we stood. It had an amazing effect. I'd heard that what you measure improves, and I saw it happen week after week. Almost immediately, as a team we witnessed undisputable evidence of our progress. Within a few months, the steady increases led to hope, and then to rock-solid trust that we were indeed on track to sustainability. Miraculously, we ended the year in the black.

What are your most important measures of success? Each business is unique, so it might take some thinking to identify your business's core success indicators for this year.

Sara started answering these questions by bringing to mind her theme—Boldly Out There. "Well, the most important thing will be to be more visible. I'd love to speak, especially at conferences. To be ready to do that though, I'd want to polish my talk. In fact, I've been dreaming of creating an e-book and now I see why. It would give conference planners a taste of my unique approach, be a great marketing piece on my website, and form the backbone of my private coaching work. To put this all into gear, I'd need to upgrade my website. Now, it's also important that I'm working with clients, because that's the point of my business. I'd like to bring on about two new clients a month and about 20 over the course of the year."

Sara landed on seven core success indicators: 1) speaking engagements; 2) new products; 3) new clients; 4) expanding her circle of relationships; 5) upgrading her website; 6) revenue; 7) her work hours and free days.

Using these as a guide, she focused all her ideas into these business goals:

- *Speaking:* Speak at 6+ conferences to audiences of ideal clients, or decision-makers.
- *Products:* Write an e-book for people with ADD describing my 6-step approach.
- *New Clients:* Attract 2 new clients a month; 20+ new clients this year.
- *Relationships:* Grow my circle of relationships from 75 to 500+ people.
- *Website:* Upgrade website to be interactive, professional and e-commerce enabled.
- *Revenue:* Generate $50,000 in revenue from coaching, speaking and products.
- *Work/Life Balance:* Work no more than 40-hours a week, with 2 work-free days a week.

Sara had identified the pivotal areas for growing the success she wants, both professionally and personally. She'd crafted goals that are concrete, measurable and anchored in time.

✍ YOUR TURN—*Your Top Business Goals*

Start by determining your core success indicators for this year. While your business is unique, some typical areas you might want to consider are revenue and profit, marketing and client attraction, new services or products, business systems, support staff, as well as your personal wellbeing and happiness.

My Core Success Indicators this year are:

_____

_____

_____

_____

You'll know when you've landed the right ones: If you focus on these your business will flourish.

Once you've mapped out your core indicators, craft a goal for each one that reflects real progress. Write a simple statement that's worded as an outcome and is concrete, measurable, time-based and inspiring.

Core Success Indicator	Goal	By when
_____	_____	_____
_____	_____	_____
_____	_____	_____
_____	_____	_____

Don't let this get too serious. Keep your goal-setting light and inspiring (just like you did when you were a kid). Map out your best understanding of what will define success now, and write it down. It's completely fine if these objectives change as you work with them. In fact I predict they will change! For now, sketch out the framework that would define success this year.

Commit and Detach

Well done. If you've captured your inspiring theme, mapped out your core success indicators and shaped them into your top business goals, you've done some tremendous work. It's time now for the final step.

Take a step back and read over your goals. I want you to ask yourself a few questions for each statement as a way to forge a whole-hearted commitment.

Do I really want this?

Your goals turn on that magic power only when they are *your* goals. You genuinely want them. They aren't someone else's good idea. They aren't what you should do. They aren't just what make logical sense. Instead, each goal reflects what *you* truly want. It's a goal worth going for. When you envision accomplishing this, do you just start smiling?

When Sara asked herself this question she pinpointed one goal she needed to toss out. "One of the on-line business gurus says that you have to post an article a week in on-line article directories in order to succeed. I'd been thinking this was one of my goals, but now I see that really it isn't. I'm just not in a place yet to generate a meaty, useful article and post it weekly. Trying to do that would be crippling, and would set back writing the e-book, which is what really matters. What a relief to just let this go. It's not *my* goal."

Do I believe I can accomplish this?

Now, I want to be clear about this question. I'm not asking if you know exactly *how* you are going to achieve this. Probably you don't. When we declare meaningful goals that create something beyond what we've done before, we most often don't know how we'll get from here to there. We're defining the end point and opening up a new learning gap. You can't know exactly how you will achieve this. What I want you to check is, do you *believe* you can achieve this? You know the feeling I'm talking about. When it's an authentic goal there's a sense you get that it's going to happen. You have the "click." If however, when you read one of your statements, it just feels unbelievable, go back and re-work it. Keep honing and shaping until you hear the signal that says, "Yes! This is a stretch, *and* I know it's doable."

Am I whole-heartedly committed to this goal?

Yes? Congratulations. As the famous quote by Goethe assures us, "Once we commit all Providence moves too."

Now, detach.

This is the paradox of masterful goal-setting. First we invest all of our heart, intelligence and energy into defining and committing to our best goals. Then, we detach and let them go.

In order to create anything in the physical world, we need to relinquish our attachment to it. When we don't, we experience the struggle, angst, and stress of "goal-itis" that I talked about earlier. We become attached to an outcome, personally identify with it and try to control life and events to conform to our picture. It's one of the most painful misunderstandings about goal-setting.

Detaching doesn't mean we give up our intention, desire and actions. What we give up is our attachment to the result. This is a very powerful thing to do. Stay highly committed to the outcome, but detach from it. To create something new means stepping out of the known to the unknown, venturing into new territory. When we detach from our goal, we are symbolically giving it over to greater creative powers beyond ourselves. Rather than trying to control or force outcomes, we are signalling our willingness to engage in the adventure of the new path we've charted.

I want to share my way of doing this, and I trust you'll find your way. After I've defined and fully committed to my goal, I end each intention by saying, "This or something better." It's a simple yet powerful symbolic act that says I've detached and let go. It's my antidote to becoming controlling, and attempting to force things in an unproductive way. I'm still whole-heartedly committed to my goal, *and* at the same time I become curious and open. Rather than becoming worried and fretting, I feel a sense of relief. I relax and feel a soul-level trust that this goal is putting into motion something beyond what I can understand right now, something that will be in my best interest and perhaps something that will be far better than I could even imagine.

 YOUR TURN—Commit and Detach

Read over each of your goals and ask yourself:

- Do I really want this?
- Do I believe I can accomplish this?
- Am I whole-heartedly committed to this goal?

Now, detach. "This or something better."

Well done! You now have the first piece of your game plan, your most important goals for this year. You've taken the crucially important step of giving shape to your inspiration. You've avoided the pitfall of becoming immobilized by an ungrounded vision. You've sent powerful new programming to your Reticular Activating System and it's already beginning to attune you to valuable information and resources that will accelerate your success. You've pinpointed the essential keys to success in your business this year. And, you've designed purpose-based goals that put your hands on the helm of your business and will allow you to steer more masterfully toward real success this year.

Next, it's time to ask the big question: Exactly *how* is this going to happen?

Vision alone isn't a roadmap. A vision without goals is a fantasy. When we confuse vision with goals we become overwhelmed and immobilized. Vision is an inspiring possibility on the horizon; goals are the concrete results we intend to achieve as we live our vision. Humans are naturally goal-oriented. A compelling goal unlocks our greater potential and leads to breakthrough results. However, we tend to avoid setting goals because it means choosing and committing, which triggers resistance. Purpose-based goal-setting is a way to avoid this pitfall and harness our creative power. You have an amazing built-in control center—your Reticular Activating System—that can help you accomplish what you want. The commitment generated when you set a compelling goal activates your RAS and programs it to bring you resources that accelerate your success. Three steps to defining your top business goals are: create an inspiring over-arching theme; craft a goal for each of your business's core success indicators; engage the full power of goal-setting by committing and detaching.

SO...HOW IS THIS GOING TO HAPPEN?

So...How Is this Going to Happen?

"Success is rarely an accident.
It is usually the result of executing a carefully
crafted set of strategies." —Jim Horan

We're at a pivotal point right now. Each step of the way—as you've tapped into your deepest commitments for your business, developed your inspiring vision and mission, and set some compelling goals— I've told you to ignore that niggling voice that asks, "But *how* am I going to do this?" That's because getting too practical too soon can hurt the process. Well, now it is time to face that question head on and come up with a winning game plan for reaching those goals.

We're going to do this in three ways. First, we'll discover your most natural and effective strategies for growing your business. Then, we'll design the high-impact action projects that will get you into motion immediately. Finally, we'll develop a realistic and inspiring money map that will guide you to financial success. When we put these three things together, you'll have a powerful roadmap for how your dream is going to happen.

Strategies: the Missing Link

I can almost hear what some of you are thinking, "Hold on. You promised no 'business-ese' and now you're talking about *strategies*!" If your eyes glazed over when you heard the words "business planning," I imagine the idea of crafting your strategies is either putting you to sleep or into a panic. Just bear with me for now, and in a few minutes I think you'll discover that you've been developing strategies for years and just haven't realized it.

A strategy, quite simply put, is a way to accomplish something. It's a broad brushstroke that defines your approach. Strategies build a bridge between your vision and where you're at today. Well-crafted strategies map out the easiest, simplest and most effective way for you to cause the outcomes you want.

If we don't define our core business-building strategies, success is hit and miss. Before I understood how to engage the power of strategies, I'd brainstorm a list of possible actions and launch out enthusiastically. But a day later, when I re-read the list, it seemed more like a morass of scattered ideas than an inviting map forward. (I bet you can relate!) Instead of setting me on a solid a path, it reduced me to confused bewilderment. I was missing the pivotal link – my core business-building strategies.

Your business-building strategies will define the shape of your business. They will state the philosophy of your company, and set the direction for your decision-making. They will design your most natural ways to market and attract clients. They will capture the most appealing and effective ways to achieve your business goals your way. Once you define your strategies you'll feel a deep confidence about how you're going to realize your business dream, and you'll have the first important part of your roadmap for growing a remarkable business.

For Shelley, the Executive Coach and Trainer we met in Chapter 2 , learning how to harness the power of strategies made a pivotal difference. She had a big dream—a world where everyone uses "coach-approach" communication skills—but even though she clearly knew her inspiring theme for this year, she was swirling in confusion. "My over-arching theme for this year is 'Take the leap.' It's time for me to move from a practice to an organization. I see such a need for these communication skills in the workplace, and I want to build a company that can make a much greater difference. But, how?" Without defining her strategies she just didn't have the decisiveness and direction to launch into potent action. The key lay in discovering her most natural business-building strategies.

How to Craft Effective Strategies

The best strategies have two key ingredients: they are based on your passion, and they leverage the best practices and trends in the marketplace. When you base your strategies on what you love doing, it's much more likely you'll actually *do* them and it's quite probable you'll *enjoy* doing them. When your strategies draw on the most successful practices in your industry, niche market and the overall market environment you'll build on the best thinking and accelerate your success.

There is no one "right way" to build a business. There is simply the way that is right for you, for your clients and for the opportunities and challenges in the marketplace now. We'll consider four key areas:

- *Your business model strategies*: the underlying design and philosophy of your business.
- *Your marketing strategies:* the ways you'll get the word out about your business and attract clients.
- *Your service delivery strategies:* your ideal methods for delivering your services.
- *Your business foundation strategies:* the support systems needed for your business (and you!) to thrive.

If you're feeling a little daunted right now, just pause and take a breath. You've already done much of the groundwork for your strategies in earlier chapters. Now you're going to build on those ideas and shape them into your most effective ways to achieve your business goals *your* way. We'll start by with a little pre-work followed by a brief visualization, and then you'll use a worksheet to crystallize your ideas into your best business-building strategies. Let's dive in.

YOUR TURN—Getting Started with Your Strategies

Your best and most natural strategies are based on your passion, and leverage what's happening in the marketplace. We'll start by recalling your passion – what you do best and love doing—and then we'll take a look at factors in the marketplace that will inform your most effective strategies.

Based on your passion

Start by taking a moment to recall your passion. Flip back to Chapter 1 where you wrote down your passion and essence statement, and if it's helpful re-write them here for easy reference.

My passionate abilities are _____, _____,

_____, _____ and _____.

My essence: I am _____.

Shelley pinpoints her passionate abilities as: natural leader, big thinker, coach-mentor and inspiring speaker, and defined her essence as 'Rainmaker & Dealmaker.' "No wonder I've felt dissatisfied for the past few years," she said. "While the core strategies I've been using—being a solo-practice and doing everything myself – made good business sense at the start-up stage, they just haven't allowed me to use my real passion. The possibility of reinventing my business to unleash my full self, is exhilarating."

Leverage Industry Trends

Your best strategies will draw on the most successful practices in your industry, niche market and the overall market place trends. Whether you've been aware of it or not, you've been gathering this information for years. Quite likely you've been doing things like observing your colleagues and competitors, listening to thought leaders in your field, or reading industry trade publications and all that thinking is just waiting for you to use now.

As a way to get started, we'll take stock of this thinking—your concerns, current trends, market challenges, as well as how you've seen others in your field overcome these difficulties.

Concerns and Challenges

What's keeping you up at night? What challenges is your business facing? What trends are affecting your ideal clients and could impact your business success? What issues in your industry and the overall marketplace do you absolutely need to consider?

_____

_____

_____

Shelley put it this way: "I see such a need for these communication skills in the workplace, but in this volatile economic climate training budgets are tighter than ever. I'm spinning with ideas, but I just don't know how I can make this leap successfully in this financially strapped marketplace."

What are others doing to overcome these challenges?

What are your colleagues and competitors doing to overcome these issues? What about their approaches appeals to you? What overall trends could you harness to uniquely position your business for success?

_____

_____

_____

As Shelley considers these questions, it gradually dawns on her that the successful industry leaders haven't been stopped by these conditions. They've been breaking the mould and using innovative techniques, like web-based learning, internet marketing, and virtual teams. "While it's true that training budgets are extremely tight that doesn't have to stop me. There are many strategies that could dramatically reduce my costs and make my programs appealing to even the most challenged budgets."

Now that you've primed the pump of your creative thinking, we'll take a few minutes to envision your best business building strategies.

 YOUR TURN—*Envision Your Natural Strategies*

Allow about 20 minutes for this and if possible, do it at a time of day when your energy is strong. Before we begin the visualization, I suggest you read over your business vision, mission and goals. When you're ready, sit in a comfortable position and allow yourself to relax. Take a few centering breaths and release the stress in your body. Feel the chair supporting you and plant the soles of your feel firmly on the floor. Take a few gentle, deep breaths and allow them to help you shift gears.

You have a unique passion. You're here to use it fully and exuberantly. Allow yourself to connect with the essence of who you are and let it fill you up right to the very cells of your body. This is the most valuable asset of your business. It is the core, the energy center, the source of boundless opportunity. Imagine this uniqueness, your authentic self, as the heart of your business. This is the base of everything. It is the base of your marketing, your services and the most enlivening way to run your business. You are aligning all aspects of your business with your passion, and tapping into a deep well-spring of energy, creativity and motivation.

There are strategies that are a natural expression of your passions. They will form the riverbed of your creativity. Just as a riverbed carves out the direction and the water flows effortlessly along, your best strategies will carve out the shape of your business, and your creative actions will flow from them with ease.

Take a breath and shift gears. Stay connected with your vibrant passion, and now expand your attention outward to include the marketplace. Over the years, whether you've been aware of it or not, you've been gathering a rich wealth of information about the best ways to connect with and serve your clients. All this information is available to you now. Bring to mind your over-arching theme and most important goals for the coming year. Fill your imagination with these rich, enlivening possibilities and breathe in the inspiration they bring to you.

Now, ask yourself the following:

What is the easiest, simplest way for me to accomplish these intentions?

What's the ideal way for me to design my business?

With my current marketing, what's the most natural way for me to get the word out about my services? What do I love doing, and how can that become my marketing strategy?

What strategies will set me up to achieve my most important goals with ease?

Just allow ideas to come to you about the most appealing, interesting and effective ways to accomplish what you want this year. There are no "right answers," only the ways that will be most natural and aligned with who you are and how you will best serve your clients. Allow yourself to hear the ideas and insights of your deeper knowing and just take note of them, however wild and unusual. Soon you will have the opportunity to sort and pick the ones you'll use.

When you feel ready, bring yourself back into the room. Breathe, stretch and shake yourself out a little. You might want to take a short break to refresh yourself before starting to write your ideas on the worksheets.

Crafting Your Strategies

We're going to crystallize the ideas you've just brainstormed into a few clear, appealing and effective ways for you to build your business. We'll start first by sketching out strategies for each of the four key areas – your business design, your marketing, your service delivery and your business foundation – and then we'll consolidate them into your core strategies.

YOUR TURN—Crafting Your Strategies:

1) Business Model: What's the ideal way for you to structure your business now? You've already thought through much of this in your business vision in Chapter 2. Take a look at it with fresh eyes and use that information along with your insights from the visualization to define the strategies that will make this business one you will love. Here are a few areas to consider. As you look at this list, see how each item could be applied to your situation and circle the ones that really jump out at you.

Solo, partner, other	Location: Home-based, downtown, other.
Fulltime or part time	Size, number of clients
Funding: self, loan, capital	Multiple streams of income

What business design strategies will set me up for success?

_____

_____

_____

As Shelley considered this, many ideas started to gel. "I could stay home-based. In the past, professionals needed a high-profile downtown office to be taken seriously. Now, we don't. If I remain home-based it would significantly reduce my overhead. As well, I've admired the way one of the leaders in my field has become a specialist in distance learning within corporations, using webinars and telephone follow-up support. What if I used a virtual approach too? Another wild idea: for the past decade I've been an advocate of the 'free agent nation' trend and have secretly fantasized about leading a company that is a virtual team of subcontractors rather than employees." Her excitement builds as she continues brainstorming strategies that combine her strengths with best practices in her field. She sketches out her business design strategies for taking the leap from a solo-practice to an organization:

- Be a home-based business to keep my overhead as low as possible.
- Leverage technology in both service delivery and marketing.
- Grow a team of collaborative associates who are licensed to facilitate and coachmy programs.

2) Marketing Strategies: A marketing strategy, quite simply put, is a way to let people know what you do. Your marketing strategies define how you'll become highly visible, build relationships, give people a taste of the real difference you can make, and attract new clients.

Your most natural and effective marketing strategies will be based on your passion. What do you most enjoy doing? Having intimate one-to-one conversations? Entertaining large audiences? Teaching classes? Building a community of like-minded people? Writing to express your unique ideas? How could this be the base of your marketing strategies? With this in mind, sketch out your marketing strategies. Here are a few areas to consider for marketing strategies:

Positioning: what do I want to be known for

Value statement

Pricing strategy: low, midrange, premium

Network/relationship/community building

Internet marketing. Social Media

Publishing: Self. Trade

Branding

Ideal client type

Introducing services

Referral sources/COI

Speaking: Paid. Free

What are my natural strategies marketing strategies? What's the most effortless and effective way to get the word out and attract clients? How will I introduce my services to potential clients? What do I want to be known for?

_____

_____

_____

Shelley started feeling a new-found liberation. "When I think of basing my marketing strategies on what I do best, it's just so clear. I love to speak, build deep and genuine relationships and write. After brainstorming a few ideas, she boiled her marketing strategies down to:

• Become known as *the* coach-approach communication company
• Launch programs with introductory live and webinar talks and workshops
• Introduce my Executive Communication coaching by offering pro-bono training/coaching to 5 leaders in my network to build reputation & referrals.
• Utilize e-marketing with a monthly e-newsletter, blog and social networking presence

3) Service Delivery: Your service delivery strategies define your ideal services and how you'll deliver them. You've already done some in-depth thinking about this when you developed your business vision. Flip back to pages 76 and 77 and read over your services, both the ones you're doing currently and the new ones you want to create. Now consolidate them into a statement or two about your strategies. Here are a few approaches to prompt your thinking:

Sell only your services   Sell other people's services

Packaging your services   Quality assurance practices

Associates/Affiliates   Licensing/Franchising

What are your ideal, unique services? What are the most interesting and effective ways to deliver them? What would stand out as exceptional services be a pleasure to do?

_____
_____
_____
_____
_____

Shelley immediately sees her service delivery strategies. "I have my core product – the coach-approach communication program. When I look at market conditions, leading-edge trends and what I most love doing, the strategy is simple. I want to re-invent my program so it can be delivered both in-person and virtually. This is really exciting." She summed up her service delivery strategy as:

- Offer live trainings, distance learning webinars and 1-1 telephone coaching to reach a local and international clientele

4) Business Foundation: Your business foundation strategy defines the infrastructure that will set up your business (and you!) to thrive. It includes your approach to support staff, systems and processes and technology. Consider:

Use of technology	Support staff: employees, subcontractors
Automation	Systems/Procedures

What infrastructure will it take for your business and you to succeed? What support will it take?

_____

_____

_____

_____

"This is tough. I've been a sole practitioner for a few years now and it's hard to even imagine what this new business will take." I encourage Shelley to just brainstorm possible approaches, and trust that it will become clearer once she starts. "Well there's one thing I'm sure about. I know I can't do this all alone. I'll have to let go of a lot of tasks I've been doing and expand my support team." She finally arrived at an idea:

- Delegate research, copywriting, accounting and marketing admin to a professional Virtual Assistant.

If you've worked through these questions and brainstormed your potential strategies, well done! If you got stuck on one or more of them, don't worry. These are big questions, and you might need some more time to reflect on them. It if helps, go for a leisurely walk and think about how you'd like your business to look, keeping these core issues in mind.

Now, I encourage you to stand back and take a deep breath. When you feel ready, your next step will be to consolidate them into a few core strategies. Read over all of your possible strategies, and then hone and simplify your ideas until you arrive at no more than nine key strategies.

My core business-building strategies are:

1) _____

2) _____

3) _____

4) _____

5) _____

6) _____

7) _____

8) _____

9) _____

Shelley summarized her core business building strategies as:

1) Become known as *the* coach-approach communication company.

2) Reach a local and international market through offering live trainings, distance learning webinars and 1-1 telephone coaching.

3) Grow a team of collaborative associates who are licensed to deliver our programs.

4) Launch Communication program through introductory live talks and webinars.

5) Introduce Executive Communication coaching, build reputation and referrals through offering pro bono services to 5 leaders in my network.

6) Utilize e-marketing with a monthly e-newsletter, blog and social networking presence.

7) Delegate research, copywriting, accounting and marketing admin to a professional VA.

8) Develop and honour life/work boundaries that keep work joyful.

Finally, use this checklist to ensure you've landed on your best, most natural business building strategies.

- When you read each strategy, does it "fit" you? Is it based on one of your strengths? Does it feel natural to you?
- Can you imagine yourself actually doing each strategy? If not, it's not *your* strategy. No "shoulds" allowed!
- Does each of your business goals for this year have a strategy? Turn to page 127 to re-read your top goals, and check that you have a strategy for each. If you discover a gap, continue developing your core strategies.

If you answered "No" to any of these questions, it's a signal that the strategy needs a little more work. You'll know you've shaped your best, most effective strategies when you feel a quiet inner assurance that this dream *can* and *will* happen.

Well done! Crafting strategies takes some deep thinking. If you've walked through these steps and written your core strategies, you've put in place pivotal groundwork for your business success. You've boldly faced the question of "how" you will achieve your dream. You've designed the first part of your roadmap for success. You've made important decisions that are probably already giving direction to your thinking.

Next we will use these strategies to unleash high-impact actions.

A strategy maps out the easiest, simplest and most effective way to accomplish your goals. You've probably been developing strategies for years and just haven't realized it. Strategies build a bridge between your goals and where you are at today. Actions without a strategy are rarely effective in the long run. Effective strategies outline your business model, set the direction, philosophy and guidelines for what your business is and isn't. Your natural and most effective strategies are based on your strengths and leverage the best industry trends and practices. Develop core business building strategies for the four key areas of your business: your business model; your marketing; your service delivery and your business foundation. Once in place they will provide a roadmap for growing your business and unleashing high-impact results.

Action Projects

"Master the art of the project."
—Michael Port

The second part of your roadmap for success, Action Projects, is the most exciting part of your VisionPlan. This is where your vision turns into the results you've been dreaming about.

Action Projects translate your strategies into actions. They define the building blocks that add up to accomplishing your goals. They put you in the driver's seat and turn the key for growing your business. And they are a powerful tool to help you overcome the biggest challenge you'll face at this point.

Think about it. How many times have you had an inspired idea, set out to do something that would make a real difference in your business, and then never saw it through (or even took the first step)? Before I harnessed the power of Action Projects, this happened to me over and over. I'd be inspired by a possibility, set out energizing goals, and map out engaging strategies. Then I'd falter. How do I start? How do I know what will produce the results I want? I'd feel uncertain and stymied. There was a disconnection between my dream and starting to take action, and I didn't know what to do about it.

In this chapter we're going to uncover what's going on when we hit this challenge and learn how Action Projects can overcome it with ease.

From Vague Hope to Solid Stepping Stones

Shelley, the Executive Coach and Trainer, had left our last meeting excited and highly motivated about taking a leap in her business. Crafting her core business strategies had given her a deep confidence that this leap could happen. However, a few days later when we spoke she sounded discouraged and disheartened. "I don't know, something is missing. I'm still confident this dream is possible, but this past week whenever I started to take action I just seemed blocked. I'm not as effective as I know I'll need to be to really do this."

She'd hit a wall. I see many versions of this play out with my clients when they feel a sense of disconnection between their goals and where they are today. Some fill the gap with hollow optimism, saying something like, "I know I will attract the results. I just trust it." Others launch into action without hesitation, but have an underlying frenzied feeling that they are missing something crucial. For a few, the wall takes the form of inaction. They decide not to do anything until they are sure they are doing the right thing. As they wait for clarity to come to them, a confidence-eroding paralysis descends.

What's going on here? You see, everything we've done so far – the dreaming, the goal-setting, the strategizing – has all come from inside of us. While some of the questions we've asked have been difficult, for the most part we've remained in the comfort of our interior world. Now it's time to take our dreams into the outer world. It's time to turn that exhilarating inner vision into action in the physical world. And that can be scary. You know the resistance we've encountered a few times before? Well, now we're really stirring it up. Action Projects are a tool that will help you build a bridge from your inner vision to effective action in the outer world.

An Action Project defines the work that needs to be done. It maps out how you'll implement your strategies. A well-designed Action Project ignites drive, motivation and focused action. Most likely you've felt this magic first-hand. I first encountered it in a 90-day fundraising campaign with the non-profit organization. It was unlike anything I'd known before! We created a clear purpose, set an audacious target, mapped out milestones and launched into action. Specific, immediate steps helped us break free of inertia quickly, and we soon tapped into an unstoppable momentum. It was thrilling, scary, and fun. Ninety days later, when we'd surpassed our fundraising target, I understood how a well-designed project could ignite extraordinary results. In the rest of this chapter I'll show you how to harness that energy for your business goals.

How to Design High-Impact Projects

An Action Project defines concrete, doable and essential steps toward your goals. From all the churning possibilities you could do, an Action Project pulls out the most important work to be done. It outlines a map of action you can start following immediately, and it provides a structure that continuously points to your next step. It has a clearly defined beginning, middle and end which help build momentum. It's also flexible and can be adapted quickly in response to unforeseen challenges or emerging opportunities.

Mastering the art of the project will cause a leap in the effectiveness (and enjoyment) of your business. As a busy business owner, you need a simple approach to designing your project plans. When you know you how to map out a project plan quickly and easily, you'll never again lose heart over the distance between your goal and where you are right now. We'll take this in three steps:

Start where you are. The first step in designing high-impact projects is to uncover where you are now. Just the way a map in a shopping mall is only useful when it has the "You Are Here" marker clearly in place, you can only design a high-impact project when you understand your current position.

Focus on what will make a pivotal difference. From all of the ideas, desires and possibilities that interest you, only a few will make a pivotal difference. The second important step is to identify the top three projects that are pivotal to real growth in your business now.

Map out an inspiring and achievable action plan. An effective Action Project outlines your best thinking about how to get from where you are today to your desired results. Just sketching out a project plan will shift you from feeling stymied to being engaged and motivated.

STEP 1: Where Am I Now, Really?

It may surprise you that the most important first step is to understand where you're at right now, and not doing this will undermine even the best strategies. You know that discouraging feeling of taking two steps forward, and then unexpectedly sliding one step back? It's usually the result of not taking the time to think honestly about your current position, and starting from there.

If just the thought of taking stock of your current situation – your assets, issues, gaping holes and all – is raising a little resistance (okay, a lot!), you are not alone in feeling this way. It takes courage and mental toughness to be able to simply acknowledge your current reality exactly the way it is. The key is to do this without blame, shame, guilt or judgement. It can be tricky to get past your internal resistance to finding out the truth about yourself and your situation in relation to your goals. When you do, however, it's an immensely rewarding experience. You'll probably find things that make your project seem more achievable. And even if you do discover unexpected bad news, ultimately that too will be beneficial. At the very least you'll no longer fear the unknown, and your new-found clarity will quite likely lead to breakthrough thinking and a feeling of empowerment. Getting real is the vital first step: it will put your feet on solid ground, open up new ideas and free up a lot of energy.

 YOUR TURN—Where Am I Now?

Pull out your top goals and strategies, read them over, and then take a moment to breathe and relax. Remember, you're looking at the cup whether it appears half full or half empty -- without shame, blame, guilt or judgement. You're simply assessing where you are right now in relation to your goals, in order to understand your starting point. We'll start by appreciating what is already present and established. Then, you'll identify what's missing, and finally you'll look for the opportunities right under your feet waiting to be harvested.

Settle back into a comfortable position in your favourite chair and say your theme to yourself. Allow the essence of it, the spirit of what you're up to, fill your imagination. Think of each of your amazing goals and imagine they have happened, they're fulfilled. Enjoy standing in this future for a moment. It can be a rich source of energy, inspiration and wisdom, and we want to tap into all of that power at this point.

Where am I, really? What's already in place? Without judgement, ask yourself, "How close am I to achieving this over-arching theme? Where am I, really?" Just take stock with the same neutral mindset as you would when looking at that "You are here" sign in the mall. Just become aware of ideas, and as you do, jot them down.

_____

_____

_____

_____

Shelley loved bringing her over-arching theme to mind: "Make the Leap." Just thinking about the possibilities for this year lifted her spirits. "I'll know I'm in a new place, that I've made the leap, when I've brought on at least one associate, when I'm delivering the program via webinar, and when I've started reaching new clients outside of my local area."

As she reflected on her current situation, she discovered she has quite a strong base already in place toward these goals. She stated her current situation and resources for achieving her goals as, "I have a high-quality coach-approach communication program with a proven track-record of results; I have a wide circle of professional relationships (about 500) and am known for delivering communication coaching that makes a measurable difference; I am a risk-taker. I thrive when I'd doing something new."

What's missing? What are my core challenges? As you consider your in-spiring desires for this year, what concerns are playing on your mind? What don't you know? What, exactly, is missing between where you are and what you want?

As Shelley probed into what's missing, she identified three core chal-lenges: "1) I don't know this new technology; I haven't even attended a webinar yet. 2) I've only worked solo. I don't know what it will take to bring on an associate. 3) I'm swamped in admins-trivia; I don't know how I'll find time to do anything beyond what I'm currently doing."

What immediate opportunities are in front of me? What resources could help you move forward? It's remarkable how powerful this question can be. It's quite possible that you have exactly what you need right now to start this project, but it's just out of view until you look for it.

When Shelley considered her immediate opportunities, she spotted two key ones: "I know at least two other trainers who are using dis-tance learning technologies in their businesses. I'm pretty sure they would agree to an informational interview. As well, I'm involved in a couple of associations of business leaders. Perhaps someone would be willing to refer me to executives in other cities as a way to break out to a national market."

STEP 2: What Projects Will Make a Real Difference in the Next 90 Days?

Now that you've pinpointed your core issues and most compelling opportunities, the next step is to brainstorm the projects you *could* do in the next three months, and then chose three that are pivotal to focus on first.

I know, for us creative entrepreneurs focusing like this can be really tough. When we dream up exciting projects, we want to do them *all* immediately. But you know what happens when we do. We become scattered, stretched too thin, overwhelmed and usually end up not accomplishing much of anything.

To harness your creative energy, you must concentrate your power. You've probably heard of the 20/80 rule, attributed to the Italian economist Pareto. He gave us the insight that 20 per cent of our actions produce 80 per cent of our best results. Using this 20/80 thinking is essential to focusing your creative energy and producing results that have real impact.

It takes a lot of self-honesty to identify what is *really* worth going for in your business. And it will take determination to avoid getting caught up in pursuing what momentarily catches your interest instead of diving into the real work that needs to be done. But you *can* develop this clarity and focus. And by defining your priority Action Projects, then following through step by step, you'll see real progress in just a few weeks.

 YOUR TURN—Brainstorming Possible Projects

Bring to mind again your inspiring theme, the challenges, opportunities and gaps you're facing. Take a breath and relax a little more. Ask yourself, "What projects *could* I do over the next ninety days? What would lead toward this success?" Fully engage your creativity and let your imagination run free. Jot down your ideas, even the wild ones, to unleash new, innovative thinking.

What projects could I do in the next 90 days? What would make a real difference and lead toward my overarching theme?

_____

_____

_____

_____

Shelley found that envisioning possible projects was no issue at all! In fact, it was effortless and fun, and she came up with a list of more than 10 exciting ideas in no time. Her list looked like this:

Take a course via webinar.	Research webinar software programs.
Take a class in internet marketing.	Re-work my website and brochure.
Hire an assistant to help do the admin.	De-clutter and reorganize my office.
Run a pilot of program via webinar.	Upgrade my marketing materials.
Launch a marketing campaign to attract more work, suitable for an associate.	Bring on an intern associate for 3 months.

Identify the 20/80 Projects

Now from all these many electrifying ideas, which matter most? Read over your list of potential projects and ask yourself, "What is the *real* work to be done in the next 90 days or so? What will make the most immediate, important difference?" What you're looking for are the three business-building projects that will spell out genuine progress in the next few weeks.

Perhaps you know immediately which are your top priority projects. Or maybe you'll need to discuss it with a business buddy or your coach. If the top three don't jump out right away, here's a prioritizing tool that might help you connect with your intuition and pinpoint the top ones quickly.

Take each project on your brainstorming list and, one-by-one, ask yourself, "On a scale of 1 to 10, with 10 being 'This project will make the most important, immediate difference,' where is this project at?" Don't over-think this. Simply write down whatever number comes to mind. After you've rated each one, stand back and see which projects rate the highest.1) Are these your top priority projects? Feel free to adjust and modify until you feel confident that you've narrowed your focus to the 20%, the three projects that will make the largest impact.

My 3 Pivotal Projects are:

_____

_____

_____

_____

_____

_____

_____

Shelley found it much tougher to choose her priority projects than it had been to think up the ideas. She decided to use the prioritizing tool, and once she rated each one using the 1-10 Scale approach, the priority projects came into view effortlessly. "When I'm absolutely honest with myself, I'm a bit surprised. The most important work to be done, the top priority, is to get more support. I must get out from under the day-to-day detail and carve out time and energy. Otherwise, I won't have the creativity or stamina to talk to potential associates or learn new technology. Shelley decided that her three most important immediate projects are:

- Hire an admin assistant for day-to-day details.
- Run a pilot webinar.
- Bring on an intern associate.

As you do this, be open to being surprised. You might find your most important priority projects are not what you first think they will be. Consider what foundation-building work will set you and your business up for sustainable growth.

Well done! If you've arrived at your top immediate projects you've done more good solid thinking than most business owners typically do. You've clearly understood where you are in relation to your theme and goals. You've pulled out the most meaningful work to be done. Next, we'll take this information and map out a project action plan that will ignite those new results you want most.

STEP 3: Create a High-Impact Project Plan

The third step is to develop a clearly defined, motivating action plan for each of your priority projects. Okay, if you just felt a pang of anxiety, relax. This won't be as hard as you might think.

You are a natural planner. Think about it: You probably used all the planning skills you'll need this morning before you left the house, without even realizing it. Did you organize your children for their day at school? Pack your briefcase and gym bag for a full work day and evening? If you did this or something similar, you've spontaneously done everything it will take to create powerful action plans:

- You intuitively framed your purpose.
- You envisioned your desired outcome.
- You mentally brainstormed the possible actions it would take and discovered a workable order.
- You thought about what might stop you and how to get around it.
- Finally, you sorted out your immediate first step and took it.

Those are the exact steps we'll use to create your Action Project plans.

Project planning doesn't have to be elaborate. In fact, a simple plan is all it takes to be effective in most cases. You need just enough clarity, specifics and good thinking for you to believe this project is achievable – to trust you *will* do it and know where to start. However, don't be deceived by the simplicity of this kind of planning and think you can skip this step and just figure out things on the fly. I'm continually amazed by how few people take the time to think through their Action Projects, and how often the resulting lack of clarity stops talented people from making their vitally needed contribution. It's essential that you block out a plan for each of your projects. When you do, you'll fully engage the power it takes to follow through and succeed. You'll feel an immediate release of tension and gain a surge of energy, confidence and enthusiasm to get into action.

We'll use a simple framework to harness your natural planning abilities and map out your plan. Many of these questions probably sound familiar; you've been asking them as you've painted the bigger picture for your life and business goals. Now you'll apply the same powerful questions as you map out specific building blocks.

- *Purpose: What is the purpose of this project?* Why are you doing this project? What are you *really* trying to accomplish? Defining the purpose will tap into a deep well of motivation, give you a trust-worthy guide for decision-making and open up your creative thinking.
- *Outcome: What is my desired outcome?* If this project goes very well, what will success look and feel like? A clear, evocative picture of the end result will turn on your Reticular Activating System,

and begin generating ideas and attracting resources to accelerate your success.

- *Actions: What will it take to achieve this?* Identifying the possible actions it will take to accomplish your desired outcome and putting them on paper will free up creative thinking, and your mind will just start filling in the gaps.
- *Barriers: What barriers (internal and external) could stop me?* Revealing the niggling "Yeah but..." voice, then engaging the problem-solving side of your brain to design ways to overcome potential obstacles, will turn doubts into building blocks toward success.
- *Milestones: What are the key steps to my desired outcome?* When you do a thorough job of emptying out all of your ideas about the steps involved in accomplishing your desired outcome, a natural organization will start to emerge.
- *First Steps: What is the very first step?* The final stage is a deceivingly simple question. What is the very first physical action? Answering and acting on this single question is the difference between *having* a dream, and *living* your dream.

 YOUR TURN—*Creating an Action Project Plan*

Set aside about half an hour to develop your first Action Project plan. I encourage you draft your first project plan quickly to help keep this process as light and effortless as possible. You can always come back later and add to it or adjust it as you gather more information. Settle into a comfortable position, take a few deep cleansing breaths and stretch a little to relax yourself. When you're ready, bring to mind your business vision and your over-arching theme for this year. Fill your imagination with these rich, enlivening possibilities and breathe in the inspiration they bring to you.

Center yourself in your True North purpose, and remind yourself of what you truly want for others. You have a unique and very needed service to bring. It makes a real and valuable contribution to others and to your community. Allow the most uplifting images of your heart's desires fill your mind and heart for a few minutes. Draw strength, energy and confidence from these deepest and sweetest commitments.

Now, start by choosing which project you'll focus on first. (It doesn't really matter which you choose, because you'll be creating a plan for each of your priority projects very soon.)

Project: _____

1. Purpose: What is the purpose of this project?

As you think of your project, ask yourself, "Why am I doing this? What am I *really* trying to accomplish? What is the purpose of this project?" Just notice what comes to mind and write it down.

Purpose: _____

Shelley decided to use the Hire an Assistant project as the focus for her first Action Project plan. The purpose came to her immediately: "The real reason I'm doing this project is to free me up for what I—and only I—can do to make the leap." She framed her project purpose as, "To free me to lead and leap."

2. Vision: What is your intended successful outcome for this project?

Imagine this project goes *very* well. What would success look like? Bring to mind a picture of what you most want. How will you feel as a result of this project? Write *your* definition of success. If you're feeling a little stuck, start by considering, "Wouldn't it be wonderful if…."

_____

_____

Shelley's definition of a successful outcome is: *An Executive Assistant who can handle <u>anything</u> that isn't my brilliance, and we work together with ease. I feel freed up and confident to make the leap.*

3. Actions: What will it take to achieve this?

Take a deep breath and relax. Continue to think of the amazing outcome you want, and ask yourself, "What will it take to accomplish this?" Imagine for a moment that you are above this scenario, and can look down on both your current reality and your desired outcome. What steps are involved to get from where you are today to the end result? Just brainstorm the various actions it *could* take without judging, evaluating, debating or critiquing the ideas.

As thoughts pop into your mind, write them down or capture them in any way that works for you (some people like to use Post-it notes, sketches, flowcharts, even storyboards). Give yourself permission to express *any* idea and trust that you'll figure out later how it fits together. At this point, don't concern yourself with whether they are the right actions in the right order. Just get them down on paper. Putting your thoughts on paper in an informal way will free up your creative thinking, and your mind will just start filling in any gaps with fresh, unique ideas.

What are the possible steps involved in creating this outcome?

1) _____

2) _____

3) _____

Shelley chose to use large Post-it notes as a way to capture her ideas. As a thought came to mind, she quickly jotted down a phrase, and stuck it on a flipchart page. She spilled out her first wave of ideas quickly, and then continued to add to it over the next couple of days. Her brainstormed list included ideas like this:

Write about what worked with my former asst.

Advertise for an assistant

Write down what I don't want to do anymore

Draft an ideal Assistant profile

Re-listen to that audio course on delegating

Talk with Linda re: her assistant

De-clutter my office

Draft a job description

Start to write my standards, procedures etc.

4. Barriers: What barriers (internal and external) could stop you?

Now, become curious about what could stop the success of this project. What is the greatest external challenge? What is the potential inner barrier? Just listen to your deepest knowing self. What resources do you have to move past these obstacles? You are much greater than any limiting pattern, or potential barrier. You have deep and rich resources to help you navigate any issues and succeed with this project. Use this worksheet to brainstorm ways you will get past these challenges.

What potential barrier could derail me?

How can I overcome this?

_____

_____

_____

"You just hit what's on my mind," Shelley said. "Whenever I've tried hiring an assistant in the past, it hasn't worked. And the barrier is *me*. I'm the problem. I just don't like letting go of control. I start thinking, 'No one does it as well as I do.' I get impatient and, before I know it, I've taken the project back. I'll have to change that pattern."

"What would overcome that? What could you add to your list of actions?" I asked. She thought a while, and framed up three new ideas for how she could succeed in doing things in a new way:

Potential barrier

How overcome this?

Not trusting my assistant to produce results the way I want.

Write a training checklist

Takes too long to train a new person.

Identify my core requirements. What am I *not* willing to train?

Fear of letting go of control.

Design an experiment. Risk letting go where stakes low. Build new skill and trust.

5. Milestones: What are the key steps to your desired outcome?

Now that you've done a thorough job of emptying out all of your ideas about the steps involved, a natural organization will start to emerge. It's time to let a logical, linear order come into focus. Look over all of the action steps you brainstormed and consolidate them into a few key milestones. If there were ten steps involved in creating a successful outcome, what would they be? Next, estimate the optimal time frame. Right now it's just a guess, but there's power in blocking out a time frame for each milestone.

What things must occur to create the final result you want? In what order must they occur? What is the optimal timeframe?

Milestone   *Optimal timeframe*

1) _____

2) _____

3) _____

4) _____

5) _____

6) _____

7) _____

8) _____

9) _____

10)_____

Shelley laid out her key milestones as:

	Desired Timeframe
Have written out the tasks I really want my assistant to take over.	in 1 week
Refresh my delegation skills by listening to audios.	by June 15
Write a position description.	by June 30
Get free of old pattern. Feel ready to collaborate with an assistant.	by June 30
Start the search process.	by July 1
Interview potential assistants.	July 1-15
Have organized basic orientation materials.	by July 21
Choose and hire my new assistant!	by July 21
New Assistant starts!	by Aug 1
Do a review of how it's going at the end of the first 30 days.	by Sept 1

It's quite likely that the steps you map out will change dramatically as you go out and take action. However, sketching out a plan to get you from where you are right now to the successful accomplishment of this project helps create a "click" of confidence and unlock an energy that will pull you forward immediately.

6. First Steps: What is the very first step?

If at this moment you could just get up and take action, what would you do? Go to the phone and call someone? Send an email? Start doing some research on the Internet or at the library? Write down the very next physical action needed to move this project forward, and envision yourself taking it quickly and effortlessly.

The first step is…

Shelley knew her first step immediately. "Starting today I'm going to take stock of every task I do to see if it's something only I can do, or if it's something I could delegate. I'll keep a notepad with me and periodically stop to notice what I'm doing. I'll really challenge myself to think about things differently, and then jot down the jobs I could give away to someone else. Just thinking about this is exciting!"

Answering this question will also help you make some bigger discoveries. You'll know immediately whether or not you're ready to start this project. If you can't state the first action step, it could be signalling that something more is needed. Perhaps more planning. Or maybe some emotional or practical support from a trusted ally to uncover what's blocking you, and how to resolve it. When you can answer this and act, you'll know you've done sufficient planning on this project, and you're on your way.

Congratulations on drafting your project plan! You now have a map of action you can start following immediately and a structure that will continuously point to your next step. More importantly, you have a simple approach to designing project plans and the confidence that you can map out a project easily and quickly. I encourage you to make time in the very near future to draft a project plan for your other two priority projects. Simply pull out a fresh worksheet and walk through the steps. Once you have simple, solid, actionable plans for these three important developmental areas of your business, you'll feel the confidence and clarity of 20/80 thinking. You'll have harnessed the power of concentration and feel a surge of creative energy.

Now that you've mapped out your highest impact projects, it's time to look at the final element of your game plan – money. In the next chapter, we'll link up your highest vision and most important commitments with the fuel that will make your dream truly possible.

Action Projects translate your strategies into actions. They define the building blocks that add up to accomplishing your goals. Action projects are a powerful tool to help you break free of resistance and get into immediate, high-impact, sustainable action. As a business owner you need a simple approach to designing project plans. When you know how to map out a project quickly, you'll never lose heart over the distance between your goal and where you are right now. You are already a natural planner and know everything it takes to create effective project plans. There are three keys to designing a high-impact project plan: start where you are; focus on what will make a pivotal difference; write out a simple, inspiring and achievable plan. Use a 90-day timeframe to make your project compelling and produce meaningful change. Use 20/80 thinking to harness the power of concentration. An effective project plan gives you a map of action you can start immediately, and it continually points to the next step. Mastering the art of the project will cause a leap in the effectiveness (and enjoyment) of your business.

Let's Talk Money

"More good works die on the drawing board
for lack of money than for any other reason."
—Source Unknown, CBC Radio Interview

The first time I heard those words they hit me like a splash of ice water. *"More good works die due to lack of money..."* I was in my car, driving to the office where I worked as the leader of a non-profit organization with a cause I passionately believed in. For the past few minutes I'd been daydreaming about our funding challenge, wondering where the money would come from. Even though I hadn't been listening to the radio interview, the words spoke directly to the gnawing question on my mind.

Would this important, needed, good work die because of lack of money?

Something woke up in me. A firm, soul-level resolve started to take shape. No, we wouldn't fold for lack of funding. I didn't know how we would cause the turnaround—I just knew that we would.

In hindsight, that moment was when I stepped up to a new maturity as a woman around money. It launched me into a dedicated search for how to break through what held me back financially. I was determined to discover how to not just survive but thrive financially as we pursued our mission.

Money. It's such an important part of our passion business. If we didn't address money it would be like leaving gasoline out of the car. Yet, I find that we passionate business owners often hesitate to talk about finances, and hold back from clearly stating our financial desires and intentions. Women especially are conflicted about stepping into their full capability as high-earners. It is vitally important to break free of whatever holds us back (men and women alike) and assume our full financial power.

After working with many people on money issues over the years, I'm convinced that this takes a two-pronged approach. We need to combine strong inner work with skillful financial abilities for real, lasting financial prosperity. The inner work involves examining and shifting our beliefs and self-image; the outer financial work is developing and mastering new skills and habits.

Many books have been written about how to succeed financially in business. Yet very few combine financial management savvy with the more emotional, even spiritual changes necessary to create a healthy, thriving business. That's what these two chapters are all about. First we will look at the mindset that will lead you to financial proficiency in your business. Then in the next chapter, we will ground your vision in a Money Map which will focus your intention, ignite a new rush of breakthrough ideas and attract the people, opportunities and resources needed for your business to flourish.

What Holds Us Back with Money?

"It's almost like money is a topic we're not supposed to talk about," Deanne the Motivational Speaker confided to me. "As women we'd rather tell you about our sex life than what we really think about money. It's still this unspoken thing, the last taboo. Yet when I *do* talk about my money concerns, the heavy meaning and charged emotions lighten up. It helps me sort out the confused messages that are holding me back from really succeeding with my business."

Most of us have some very mixed messages about money, success and business. In my case, from a young age I heard, "You're very creative; you'll never make a living with it." While I'm sure my parents were very well-meaning, just wanting to help me have a secure future, that mixed message caused a lot of chaos in my career path. I'd vacillate between doing work I loved—but making practically no money—and making very good money but feeling unhappy doing the work. I was playing out the early programming from my childhood. It was when I started to question and break free of that core message that I discovered I could cultivate a mindset that supported me in living my deepest commitments and thriving financially.

Over the years, as I've worked with women in a wide range of passion businesses all over the world. I've heard common themes that block us from realizing our full potential financially in our business. Whether at the start-up stage or growing their business into their dream enterprise, women share similar self-sabotaging concerns. Simply hearing the doubts that many of us struggle with can have a healing and transforming effect. As I share these common challenges, I invite you to consider which might have you in their grip, and soon we'll look at how you can free yourself of them.

I never thought I'd be in business, and I'm daunted by the financial side. I feel lost.

Many of us struggle with a self-image that says "business just isn't for me." Women often tell me they never imagined they'd be in business. No women in their immediate or extended family were in business, and they just assumed they would always be an employee. Entrepreneurism is all new ground, and without some kind of roadmap we feel lost.

Is doing what I love for a living <u>really</u> work?

Many of us have dreamed of doing what we love, but never really believed we would make our living at it. We are haunted by a niggling question about the validity of making our passion our work.

If I can do this, can't everyone? It's hard to value this when it's so effortless.

When we are doing what we love, what we are meant to do, it often comes so naturally it feels effortless. When our work flows with such ease, I've heard repeatedly, "If I can do this, can't anyone? What real value can this have if this is so effortless for me?"

I don't know how to charge when I'm the service.

Setting fees in a service business is entirely different than with a product-oriented business where there is a pre-set fee or established formula. It can be difficult to have an objective perspective when we *are* the service. Designing our fees gets even more complicated when our pricing gets tangled up with our self-worth. On a good day we trust we're competent professionals with a service that has real value. However, on a day when the wind has been knocked out of our sails, it can be hard to believe we're worth anything at all.

If I raise my rates, I might lose clients. I just don't want to risk the relationship.

As purpose-led entrepreneurs, we care deeply about our clients. We have a heart-to-heart connection with them, which we try to shield from money concerns. This hidden conflict shows itself most noticeably when it's time to raise our rates. We may even avoid the issue without knowing why.

We're in tough economic times. Maybe I can't succeed in this climate.

Daily we are bombarded with newscasts reporting new crises, unprecedented changes and predictions of a dire future. They can rock us to our core and shake the confidence of even the most seasoned business owner. Fear can take over like a flu virus. Suddenly we are caught in the grip of scarcity thinking, plagued by thoughts like *'There's not enough.' 'There won't be enough work for my business.' 'I'm not enough to cope with this.'* When we let this kind of thinking take over, negative expectations become self-fulfilling prophesies.

Really, just who do you think you are?

Over and over I've seen it in myself and my clients. As soon as we get serious about stepping into a greater expression of our contribution—whether it is boldly offering a new service, moving our rates up or deciding to completely re-invent our business to play our biggest game—the critical voice gets louder and louder challenging us by saying "Just, who do you think you *are*?"

YOUR TURN – Money Messages

Which of these challenges has you in its grip? Pause for a moment and take stock of the fears that plague you most about succeeding financially in your business.

- I never thought I'd be in business and I feel daunted and lost.
- Is doing what I love for a living *really* work?
- I don't know how to charge when *I'm* the service.
- It's hard to value this when it's so effortless.
- If I raise my rates I'll risk the relationship.
- These are tough economic times. Maybe I can't succeed.
- I suffer from the nagging voice that says "Really, just who do you think you are?"

What other money messages are holding you back? Whether rational or not, write down all the reasons money is stopping you from growing your business (or getting it started).

Be as negative as you want. By the end of the chapter, you'll see that most of it doesn't actually apply to your situation, and the rest can be solved with a shift in your approach.

_____

_____

_____

_____

_____

_____

_____

A New Money Mindset

"Our problems cannot be solved at the same level of thinking we were at when we created them." —Albert Einstein

I've come up with seven shifts in mindset about these challenges that will free up your innate ability to prosper in your business, whatever the economic climate. Some of them you probably already have in place; others might seem quite new, perhaps even completely opposite to what you've heard. As we look at each one, try them on to see how they might free up your entrepreneurial creativity and grow your financial potency.

I never thought I'd be in business and feel daunted and lost.	→ Realize that you are pioneering new ground.
Is doing what I love for a living really work?	→ Value your unique contribution and take a stand on your business.
I don't know how to charge when I'm the service.	→ Disentangle your self-worth from money.
It's hard to value this when it's so effortless.	→ Get over "struggle" and allow yourself to be well-paid
If I raise my rates I'll risk the relationship	→ Reconcile money and love.
These are tough economic times. Maybe I can't succeed.	→ Cultivate a prosperity mindset.
Really, just who do you think you are?	→ Step up to your true power.

Realize that you are pioneering new ground

If, at times, you feel like you're on completely new terrain, perhaps it's because you are. Historically, business and earning money is still very new ground for women. It wasn't until the Second World War that women in the workforce was the norm. In the 60 years since then, the progress of women in the workplace has been uneven at best. Barbara Stanny in her book *Secrets of Six-Figure Women* quotes a 1999 study by Deloitte Touche which reports that it has only been the last two decades that women have had substantial personal earnings from their own activities. Women earning six-figures or more are still in the minority. Fewer than 20 percent of six-figure earners are female.

For most of us, this means that we are pioneers. We haven't benefited from the mentoring of other women about earning money through our contributions in the marketplace.

This really hit home for me when I heard Dr. Christina Northrop, a leading authority on women's issues, interviewed about her book on women and their mothers. She commented that one of the issues for our generation of women is how to 'be' in the world. Our mothers may have been just the first generation of women in the workplace. This meant we had little modeling and sometimes received mixed messages about women as contributors in the world. Some mothers were overly protective, fearing for us, not wanting us to get hurt in the world. Others, who perhaps wished that they had had those opportunities, were unconsciously comparing and competing. Hearing this helped me realize that as a women business owner, I am a leader cutting new ground in the world of work and money. I granted myself a new level of compassion, made a firm commitment to become more masterful with business, and sought out mentors for both emotional and practical support.

If you're struggling with a self-image that says "business just isn't for me," know that entrepreneurism for women—especially in a passion businesses—is all new ground. Give some thought to what support you really need to build your business skills and financial literacy. Invest in building your knowledge and capacity through taking classes or reading books. Consider what emotional and leadership development support would accelerate your success and seek out a business mentor or a coach.

What do you need to learn to be financially literate? What support—emotional, financial or in leadership development—would benefit you most? Who would you love to have as a mentor or coach with this?

Value your unique contribution and take a stand on your business.

Doing what you love for a living is *real* work. In fact, it's what you are meant to do and is the best way to make your greatest contribution. However, there is a key question you'll need to answer. Do you intend to make your unique contribution as a business or a hobby? There are many valid ways to use your gifts in service of others. Some people do it as a hobby. Some do it as a volunteer project. Others choose to create a business as their vehicle for contributing to others. If your dream is to run a flourishing, profitable passion business, it's essential that you take a stand on your business success and eliminate any doubts about mixing passion and business.

"This was a turning point in my financial success," Shelley said. "You see, when I worked in corporate, my secret passion had been to uncover the keys to compassionate, collaborative communication in the workplace. When I started my communication business and got to do this full time it felt like a delicious indulgence. I even felt a little guilty. When friends and colleagues asked me when I was going to get a *real* job, I didn't know what to say. The breakthrough moment came when my coach asked me if this was a hobby or a business. A light came on and I realized *I* needed to validate this as real work and treat it with the same commitment and professionalism I'd shown my best clients in the past. Once I took this stand, it didn't matter if others questioned what I was doing. I had unshakable confidence that this was real and very important work. It's funny, very soon afterward a new level of clientele and revenue came into my business."

If questions about whether this is *real* work still haunt you, it's time to choose. Is this a business, or a hobby for you? If it's a business, take a stand on your business success and close the door on any thinking that you're diminishing your value or treating your business as less than professional.

> *Is your dream to run a business? Or is this a hobby? If it's a business, how are you still treating it as a hobby? What changes is it time to make?*

Disentangle self-worth from money

Your worth as a person can never have a price tag. Your services, however, must. To be effective in designing and pricing your services, you must distinguish between who you are—your personal worth as a human being—and the value of the services you offer.

When Marie, the Personal Chef, heard these words she breathed a sigh of relief. "Now I understand why I struggled so much with setting my fees when I first started out. I'd designed a great introductory pricing strategy—a reduced-fee to my first 10 clients—as a way to introduce my services and attract those important first few clients. But I felt a knot of resistance in my stomach every time I offered it. Now I see I was getting all confused because I thought a low fee meant something about my personal worth. When I get my self-esteem out of the equation it is much simpler and more straight forward. My fee is just a number, and I can change that number as my skills improve, as my reputation grows or my target market changes."

If you're held back by this, know that you are a priceless human being. Do the inner work needed to detach your self-image from your business results and invest the time needed to strengthen your authentic self-esteem. When you do, your fees will simply be fees and you'll have the freedom to design the pricing that best serves your business and your clients.

What do you need to do to disentangle your self-esteem from your fees,
once and for all? What changes is it time to make with your fees?

_____

_____

_____

_____

_____

_____

Get over "struggle" and allow yourself to be well-paid.

Doing what we love comes naturally. The closer you are to your sweet spot, the easier it is. When I first realized that , I actually felt uncomfortable. I'd tripped over a lurking message saying "You have to work hard for the money." If you absorbed that old belief too, I want you to turn it on its head. It's time to give up the ingrained pattern of struggling and suffering to validate what you do.

Kristin, the personal trainer, actually doubted whether her services would be as valuable if she wasn't working hard and struggling. As an experiment, for a week she stopped doing intense preparations before client appointments and just 'showed up,' trusting that she would intuitively know what to do with her clients. "You know, it's been interesting this week. I've felt much lighter, and actually had fun. But what amazed me was that my clients didn't notice that I hadn't prepared. Actually, I think I connected with them more because I was right there in the moment with them. It kind of rocked my world to think that my work could be this effortless and even more effective."

Is it okay for you to be paid well to do what you love? If you find yourself in a quandary about this, there are two steps that can help you break out of it. First, get the focus off yourself and onto the value of your services for others. Second, look for other talented people who are charging well for their services. "When you say that, I think of my hairdresser," Kristin said. "I go to a very expensive hair stylist. He loves styling hair, but he charges for it. I wouldn't expect him to cut my hair for free just because he loves doing it. So why should I get knotted up in thinking I shouldn't get paid well for my services!"

Is it okay for you to be well-paid doing what you love? If not, what steps can you take to resolve this quandary about being well-paid for what comes naturally to you?

Reconcile money and love

Those of us in a service business must reconcile caring for our clients and charging money. This is especially important in a service business— more so than if we were selling a product—because our services come from who we are and connect with who our clients are. It's a heart-to-heart connection. We are people who care for people, and this can get confusing when we add money into the mix.

When we were discussing setting her fees, Sara, the ADD Coach who loved teaching people to minimize their symptoms and enhance their real strengths, asked me point blank: "What is this? Am I charging for my love?" "Well, not really," I said. "Look at it this way: You're charging for your skills. You're charging for your time. You're charging based on the value your services provide for others. The love is free."

There is no one right answer to this dilemma, however it is very important that you do resolve this issue in a way that makes sense to you. If you're conflicted about caring for your clients and charging money, talk it over with another business owner who has reconciled money and love until you feel peace about both caring for your clients and charging well for your services.

How do you reconcile money and love? If you're still confused about charging for your services, who could support you in resolving this so that you feel at peace with your fees?

_____

_____

_____

_____

Cultivate a prosperity mindset.

In the midst of uncertain economic conditions it's understandable to question whether we can succeed. There is so much we can't control— local conditions, world events, the actions of our clients. But there is something we can always control: Our ability to do the one thing that changes everything. We can take charge of our own mind. We can choose whether we get caught up in a trance of fear and scarcity thinking, or whether we view our world with a prosperity mindset. As a creative entrepreneur, I imagine you've experienced the power of a prosperity mindset many times. It's an abiding sense of optimism. A bone-deep knowing that, despite appearances, there is always a new potential ready to emerge. A trust that this is an abundant universe and we are enough to accomplish what we're meant to do.

Julie, the business coach, recently faced the choice between scarcity thinking and a prosperity mindset head-on. "A third of my clients ended our sessions after a month. While each ending was healthy, a result of the client succeeding with their goals, it knocked the wind out of my financial sails. As well, it was the beginning of summer, my slowest time of year for generating new business." She faced a crucial choice. Give in to an under tow of scarcity and fear and inaction, or meet this challenge with a prosperity mindset. When she honestly admitted her fear it began to dissolve, and something else emerged. "A quiet, deeper voice seemed to be assuring me that these endings were in fact clearing the way for something new. Though it took a deliberate choice—sometimes many times a day—I gradually felt the fear replaced with a sense of curiosity, then trust that something new was on the way." Julie had broken free of automatic scarcity thinking. Now, let me be clear. A prosperity mindset isn't magical thinking. She didn't passively wait for something to happen, or leap headlong into risks uninformed about real market conditions. She coupled her mindset of positive expectancy with intelligent research and daily marketing actions. She launched a new service and within six weeks her client portfolio was again full. And she'd forged an even stronger prosperity mindset. Choice by choice she'd engaged from a sense of wholeness, positive expectancy, creativity and trust in the goodness of life, even in the face of adversity.

Cultivating a prosperity mindset is one of the most important acts you can take to ensure your success in uncertain economic times. Just like Julie, you will grow it choice by choice, in the seemingly small daily actions in your business—taking the risk to launch a new service in the midst of an economic downturn, bidding on a new piece of work even when it's a stretch to deliver, or quoting your full fees rather than selling short from fear. You can take charge of your mindset, whatever the circumstances, and use each challenge to cultivate a deep, unshakable prosperity mindset.

When you're really honest with yourself, what effect has the economic turmoil had on your confidence to succeed? Have you ever experienced the power of a prosperity mindset? What if you lived from this stance in your life as the norm, no matter what's happening? What actions could you take to foster this mindset?

Step up to your true power

There are, as we've seen, many reasons why women have difficulty fully succeeding financially in their passion businesses. More often than not, all the reasons boil down to one pivotal factor. The fear of our own power. For us to fully succeed in our business, (yes, financially too) it means claiming and becoming comfortable with our power. And this is new territory.

Historically, women have been the supporters, the caregivers to others. We have tended to nurture and support others—our children, husbands, people in power—in achieving their dreams. There is nothing wrong with this, as long as we aren't doing it at the expense of our own lives. Unfortunately many of us have found we've gradually taken a back seat to others, stunted our own growth for their benefit, and even lost our authentic self in the role of supporter.

"This is a little hard for me to hear," Deanne, the Motivational Speaker told me. "But you're describing exactly what happened to me. After a decade of taking care of my children and husband, I felt like my life revolved around them. I loved taking care of them, don't get me wrong, but it was like I'd lost something along the way. It was like I'd become a satellite around their lives. My identity, my sense of value and worth, was a reflection of their successes. And, there was some kind of unspoken agreement there too. An unconscious contract that went something like, 'If I take care of them, I'd be taken care of.' It's very tough to admit, but deep down inside, I have a rescue fantasy. I want someone to take care of me."

It takes immense courage, honesty and determination to break free of this message and unconscious contract. It takes tremendous bravery and unwavering self-honesty to accept full responsibility for your results in business and life, no matter what. As you give up the erroneous expectation that someone will always be there to take care of you, you become free to claim your real power which has been lying dormant. When you live from this stance, you will awaken personal leadership and unlock your true potential. You were born to use your creative power. It's who you are. You were never meant to be someone's moon; you are a sun with your own brilliant potential ready to shine. While you might feel some trepidation about owning your personal authority, it is the beginning of claiming your enormous capacity to influence and make your full, unique and needed contribution in this world.

> *Have you become a satellite to others? Or are you a sun radiating your own unique brilliance? What is next for you to claim your authority and step fully into your power?*
>
> _____
>
> _____

Assessing the Money Mindset Shift

Making these seven shifts will free up your entrepreneurial creativity and grow your financial potency. We've covered a lot of ground in the last few pages and it's quite likely it's stirred up some uncomfortable feelings. If so, take a deep breath and relax. Seeing old patterns and constricting messages is the first step in freeing yourself from their grip. In this next activity, you'll turn around the money messages that have been holding you back and author your new soul-level stance on money, one that will unlock your ability to thrive financially as you pursue your mission.

> *Your Turn—Take Charge of Your Money Mindset*
>
> You have the ability to take charge of what you're telling yourself and author a money mindset that is profoundly empowering. As you engage in this activity, I encourage you to be compassionate, gentle and kind with yourself. As we said earlier, money is the last taboo, and taking charge of that mindset can challenge you to your very core. Take it step-by-step, and if at any time you feel overwhelmed, just stop and take a break. Breathe. Walk around. Stretch. Do whatever restores your energy and perspective. While this work can be tough, it's also very liberating.

Look back over what you've written about your limiting money messages (on page 172) and review any notes you've jotted down as you read each of the shifts. Now, one by one, examine each of your limiting money messages and challenge them. See if you can uncover a deeper truth, one that is *really* true for you and craft new empowering statements that help you break free of the old disempowering message.

Once you've defined your new stance with money, map out a few key actions that will build your financial skills and capacity.

This work is the starting point of establishing your new maturity as a woman around money.

Note: If you find it difficult to turn around a debilitating message, turn to page 219 for a step-by-step process for transforming limiting messages.

My New Money Mindset

What money messages is it time for me to release? What money mindset would empower me to fully thrive and flourish in my business?

_____

_____

_____

_____

Actions that will increase my financial literacy and capacity with money.

What is it time to learn about the financial side of your business? What actions could grow your financial proficiency?

1) _____
2) _____
3) _____
4) _____
5) _____

Here are a few examples of money statements to get you started.

- As a woman business owner, I am a pioneer in the world of women, work and money. I am leader cutting new ground. I am capable of growing my capacity with business and money. I am on a path of mastery and can learn everything I need to flourish in my business.
- Doing what I love is *real* work. I value my passion and unique contributions. This is a real business and I choose to bring my best to my work.
- I am not my business or my fees. I am a worthwhile, valuable human being simply for who I am. My fee is just a number and I can change that number when it's time to make a change. My fee reflects the value of my services to my clients.
- My work can be effortless *and* highly effective.
- It's okay for me to be well-paid for what comes naturally and with ease.
- It's okay for me for me to be a high-earner doing what I love doing.
- I am stepping into my full capability as a high-earner now.
- I charge for my skills; I charge for my time; I charge based on the value my services provide for others. The love is for free.
- I am the chooser. No matter what challenge I'm facing, I can take charge of my mind.
- I choose to release fear and become curious about what wants to happen here.
- It is an abundant universe. There is enough for everyone.
- I am enough to accomplish my purpose and live a life I love.
- I am enough, and I have access to all I need right now in this moment.
- I was born to use my creative power. It's who I am. I am a sun, meant to shine.
- Power is not power over others. Power is the ability to co-create *with* others.
- I am 100% responsible for the results in my business and life. I can learn and grow from my results. They are a valuable teacher.
- Money can be a mirror of how I'm expressing my power and making a valuable contribution to others.

If you have crafted your new, empowering money messages and laid out your action plan for growing your financial savvy, well done! This is very challenging work and few people actually engage deeply enough to claim their power in relation to money. You've begun to put in place essential groundwork that will ensure your highest aspirations in business and life are fully funded.

Your next step will be to harness one of the most important money skills there is—developing a Money Map for your VisionPlan. It will focus your intention, give you a roadmap to steer your business to financial success, and ignite a new rush of breakthrough ideas, people and resources to help your business flourish.

Money is an important part of succeeding with your passion business. Without financial proficiency your business and mission are at risk of failing. Succeeding financially in your business takes both inner and outer work. Many of us have very mixed money messages that keep us from stepping into our capabilities as earners. You can cultivate a money mindset that will free your entrepreneurial creativity, grow your financial potency, and ensure your highest aspirations in business and life are fully funded.

Harness the Power of a Money Map

*"Clarity leads to power, the ability
to create what you really want."*
—*Marshall Thurber*

There is one final, vitally important step to your VisionPlan—grounding your dream in a Money Map.

A Money Map is a tool that translates your business vision into a financial roadmap for a thriving and profitable business. Putting your financial plan on paper is a way of visioning. It pulls all of the pieces together and sets a clear financial path to your goal.

Learning how to design and then lead your business from a Money Map is an essential skill for us passion-business owners. You might already have a financial planning method that works well for you and if so, I encourage you to use it. But if you've never created a financial plan, or if you find traditional budgeting methods just don't fit for you, I want to offer you a simple seven-step process that has done wonders for many of the passion-business owners I work with.

Why Do We Get Stuck When it Comes to Financial Planning?

Let's be honest. Getting specific about money and putting numbers on paper is one of those activities that makes house cleaning look fun. Many of us zone out, perpetually 'forget' or are always just 'a little too busy' to map out the financial side of our business dream. I hear comments like these:

"I don't want to be that anal. I want to just let the money flow."

"A financial plan is too restrictive. I'm just too creative for financial planning."

"I put a lot of time into making a plan last year, and I didn't hit my numbers. Why bother?"

"Writing a financial plan is too complex. I don't understand it. I'm not a numbers person."

"How can I create a money plan when the economy is this uncertain? I can't know what's going to happen."

Developing a Money Map *can* be daunting. One of the reasons it's so challenging is that it triggers a cascade of doubts, fears and negative chatter. As I've worked with money mapping, both with myself and my clients, I've grown to understand that this is *precisely* why it is such a powerful tool. When we are brave enough to paint a picture of succeeding financially, and are willing to face the resistance that surfaces, we can address these issues before they undermine our success. In fact, a future chapter will show you specific ways to transform any limiting thinking that emerge as you design your Money Map. For now, I want you to trust that you can do this. Even if you feel uncomfortable, know you are on a direct path to transforming your resistance into exactly what you'll need to grow a thriving, prospering business.

Deanne, the Motivational Speaker whose dream is to use her creativity much more in her work, was highly skeptical when I first suggested developing a Money Map. "I understand what you're saying, but that's just not for me. I'm too creative, just not a numbers person. When I've tried to get some numbers on paper in the past I've just kind of zoned out. And, with the nature of my business, it's all just too unpredictable to create a budget or financial roadmap." Though she was resisting the idea, she was also very committed to her dream and willing to learn whatever was needed to succeed. Over the next few pages you'll see how Deanne courageously painted her unique picture of flourishing financially. In the process she unlocked a remarkable power to have money serve her higher mission.

✍ YOUR TURN—What Could Stop You?

When you think of creating a Money Map for your business dream, what comes to mind? Excited anticipation? Dread? Can't do it? Don't want to?

_____

_____

_____

_____

_____

Whatever your thoughts are right now about creating a money map for your dream, I want to assure you that you *can* do this. Take the rest of this chapter step-by-step and give yourself complete permission to take a break whenever you need to. Soon you will have the skills to develop a Money Map whenever you need one, and you'll have a roadmap to personal and business viability.

What Happens If You Don't Have a Money Map?

Running a business without a Money Map is like walking in the woods without a compass: Your vision may be very clear, but if you don't know exactly where you're headed, there's no way to gauge your progress. You'll feel lost when things don't go the way you expect, and it will be hard to make decisions because you won't have the concrete numbers you need to choose wisely. Without a Money Map, you might be busy, you might even have a gush of revenue, but you won't know if you're making any real progress toward a financially successful business.

The act of creating your Money Map signals that you are serious about your dream. When you translate your Action Projects into concrete numbers and determine what resources you need to succeed, it's a powerful statement that you mean business. This isn't a hobby any more, something you will do if you feel like it, or if everything goes well. You're taking 100% responsibility for your business success.

Crafting a Money Map puts gas in the tank of your dream. It brings rock-solid clarity, the kind that evokes a new inner power. Thinking through the numbers forges a clear intention and sends a directive to your unconscious that ignites a rush of creativity and new ideas; and it has the uncanny effect of attracting the opportunities, resources and people to make your vision really happen. Taking the time to develop a comprehensive, simple Money Map will be as illuminating and useful in guiding you toward a profitable business as that compass in the woods.

"You know," Deanna said, "I like that you're not calling this a budget. Just hearing the word 'budget' makes me cringe, makes me feel pressured and anxious. A budget sounds like something that's set in stone, that's restricting, and my creativity just dries up. Calling it a Money Map makes me think of a tool that will guide me to where I really want to go. I feel freed up, intrigued and engaged. It's actually sparking my creativity."

How to Develop Your Money Map

You don't need to be an accountant or financial wizard to create your financial plan. While you might want to get the counsel of a trusted financial advisor, I believe it's important for you as a business owner to be able to develop (and then lead) your business from a plan that makes sense to you. Most budgeting software and templates are overkill for us passion-business owners. It is possible to create a meaningful and potent Money Map on one page with the financial skills you have now.

There are seven steps to creating your Money Map:
1. Start by defining your personal financial needs
2. Map out your business' financial needs
3. Set your revenue target
4. Brainstorm your earning plan
5. Pull everything together into your Money Map

6. Embrace and transform any emotional "chatter" this has triggered

7. Use your Money Map to steer your business to prosperity

Let's walk though each one of these and apply the steps to your business vision.

STEP 1: Define Your Personal Financial Needs

What amount of money do you need personally to thrive in your life?

Your business is meant to serve your life priorities and, just as we did earlier when you set your vision, we are going to start first by defining your personal financial needs. Often, we business owners think in terms of getting to keep 'what's left over' after everyone else is paid. I want you to turn this thinking around and put yourself and your needs first. When you do, you will create a business that takes care of your deepest commitments and is a vehicle for achieving your definition of success.

Perhaps this number is already clearly in focus for you. I find though, when I am supporting clients in creating their Money Map, they are usually vague about the amount of money it takes for them to be financially fit. If you haven't defined this recently, your first step is to bring it into focus. You might need to track your expenses for a few months to get a handle on the cost of your current lifestyle. If you are in a committed relationship, this might involve a conversation with your partner about how you are collaborating financially.

Now if, as soon as I mentioned tracking your expenses, you started feeling tired or had a sudden urge to grab a magazine to find out which movie star just got married, take a deep breath. It's true that this can be tough to do. However, it's not as hard as you think and the work will be well-worth the effort. Taking care of yourself financially is a key form of self-love. You can do this and it's vitally important that you learn this skill as part of taking charge of your business and your life. Take a deep breath, and let's dive in.

YOUR TURN—STEP 1: Your Personal Financial Needs

What amount of money do you need to thrive in your personal life? As you read through Deanne's example, start sketching out your financial needs.

When I first asked Deanne what amount of income she needed to thrive personally, she was surprised and a little embarrassed. "I haven't thought of it this way. I haven't been separating my personal finances from my business finances. You know, I don't know exactly what my personal financial needs are. I'm one of those people you described. I thought I needed to 'make do' with what's left over. I hadn't realized I was so vague about this." These insights prompted a complete financial review, including conversations with her partner. After a few weeks, she came to our session with a sense of peace. "This took some digging and some courage, but it is *so* worthwhile. I now know what I need as my salary to be successful in my life. At first it was difficult to face the reality of what I really need, but now that I'm clear, I feel empowered and somehow more confident that my business can and *will* provide what I need to live the life I love." Her personal spending plan looks like this:

Deanne's Personal Spending Plan	Monthly	Annual
Home (Mtge, Utilities, Ppty tax, telephone Home Insurance, Maintenance, Cable)	$1,235	$14,820
Food (Groceries, Eating Out)	400	4,800
Self-care (Health & Beauty supplies, massage, Medicine, Dental Care)	250	3,000
Clothes	100	1,200
Insurance: Life	125	1,500
Fun/Recreation/Entertainment	100	1,200
Children (no longer live at home)	100	1,200
Weekly Cash	300	3,600
Vacation	100	1,200
Gifts (Birthdays, Christmas)	130	1,560
Charitable Contributions	75	900
Retirement Savings	300	3,600

Debt Repayment (credit cards)	100	1,200
Bank Charges	30	360
Subtotal	**$3,345**	**$40,140**
Taxes (Federal & State/Prov)	900	10,800
Government Withholdings	200	2,400
Total	**$4,445**	**$53,540**
TARGETED SALARY:		**$55,000**

Of course, each of us is unique. Your lifestyle commitments, stage of life, geographic location, etc. will inform the expenses in your life. This example is for illustrative purposes only, not to suggest what you're spending plan should be.

Once you've calculated your personal financial needs, you have the information you'll need to determine your targeted salary in your business.

STEP 2: Map Out Your Business' Financial Needs

Next we'll outline the estimated costs involved in running your business this year (or whatever timeframe makes sense to you). We'll approach it in two broad brush strokes. First you'll define your basic ongoing expenses. Then you'll outline your project expenses.

Your basic ongoing expenses are the costs involved in operating your business. One way to think of this is to imagine when you wake up tomorrow morning, what expenses would be involved in running your business before you do anything new or different?

Every business is unique, so these expenses vary from business to business. Some typical, ongoing expenses of a passion-business include rent, telephone, internet charges, auto, office equipment, etc.

The Project and Discretionary Costs are the expenses involved in implementing your Action Projects, the new work that will grow your business.

While this approach—separating ongoing expenses from project expenses—might be different from traditional accounting methods, I have found it puts us in charge of our decision-making about spending. Month-by-month we can adjust our choices in response to our revenue, and stay in charge of profitability through ebbs and flows.

🖋 YOUR TURN—STEP 2: Your Business' Financial Needs

a) Basic Ongoing Expenses

What are the basic, ongoing expenses of your business? As you read through Deanne's example, let it spark ideas as you draft your ongoing expenses. There are no "right" categories, simply the ones that apply to your unique business.

When Deanne considered her business' financial needs this way a light bulb came on. "You know, I've just lumped everything together and spent money on things as I needed to. Now I'm seeing there are regular expenses involved in just operating my business, and then there are the costs of my current projects." Her Basic Expenses Worksheet looks like this:

Deanne's On-going Business Expenses	Monthly	Annual
Administative & Financial		
Accounting	$250	$3,000
Bank Service Charges	15	180
Virtual Assistant	150	1,800
Total Admin & Fin Exp	**$415**	**$4,980**
Auto/Transporation Exp		
Auto Loan	$300	$3,600
Gas & Oil	100	1,200
Insurance	150	1,800
Parking	25	300
Repairs & Maintenance	85	1,020
Total Auto Expenses	**$660**	**$7,920**

Computer & Office Exp		
Computer Supplies	$50	$600
Internet Charges	50	600
Cell Phone Charges	50	600
Office Rent	200	2,400
Office Supplies	75	900
Total Comp & Off Exp	**$425**	**$5,100**
Marketing		
Website: Hosting & Maintenance	$50	$600
Memberships: Assoc; Networks	25	300
Materials	100	1,200
Total Marketing	**$175**	**$2,100**
Payroll		
Gov't W/H	$75	$900
Critial Illness Insurance	150	1,800
Healthcare Insurance	350	4,200
Wages/Salary	4500	54,000
Total Payroll	**$5,075**	**$60,900**
Professional Development		
Classes, training, coaching	$300	$3,600
Total Prof Dev	**300**	**3,600**
Total	**$7,050**	**$84,600**

b) Project and Discretionary Expenses

Take a breath and walk around. Drilling down and getting a clear picture of your business' needs can be challenging work. When you're ready to start again, we'll estimate the costs you expect will be involved in implementing your Action Projects. Begin by looking back at the priority Action Projects you defined on page 157. List your projects for the coming year (or use a shorter timeframe if that makes more sense to you). One by one, estimate what costs you foresee will be involved in each of these projects.

Deanne felt a new-found clarity as she tackled this section of her Money Map. "At the moment my number one priority project is writing a book, which involves paying an editor, a word processor and a graphic artist. My other two priority projects for the next six months are upgrading my business foundation—buying a new computer and PDA—and reworking my website to be able to sell products on-line. Looking at this section of my Money Map as initiatives will let me adjust how quickly I implement these plans. If I have the money, I know what I can do this month. If I don't I can wait. I'm getting a clearer sense of what's immediate and what's down the road. I feel much more in charge." Deanne defined her plan this way:

Deanne's Discretionary/Projects Expenses (January to June)

		Monthly	6 months
Book:	Editor	250	1500
	Cover Design		500
	Layout		1500
Business Foundation Upgrade			
	New Computer		1200
	PDA: iPhone		300
	Operating fees	50	300
Website Upgrade			
	E-commerce enabled		350
	Monthly revisions	100	600
Subtotal			**$6,250**

STEP 3: Set Your Revenue Target

Now, let go of everything you've done so far. Set aside all the information you've generated about costs. Our next step is to discover your ideal revenue target for this year, and we'll be doing it in a slightly different way from traditional revenue forecasting. Instead of analyzing and calculating, you'll start first by listening to your intuition. It's uncanny how a wise part of you already knows what's just right for you this year.

 YOUR TURN – STEP 3: *Your Revenue Target*

Take a deep breath and stretch your body to help you relax. With your next breath, go to your heart and invite in your wise, knowing self. Take a few minutes to think about your business. Bring to mind your business vision, your mission, the ripples of impact your work could have. Allow yourself to be in this extraordinary future you intend to create.

Now, I have a question for you. If this all happened, what amount of money would it generate? Allow a number to come to mind. Don't over think it. Just allow the number to come.

Got it?

It might make you gasp a little. Or it might feel very comfortable and doable. Just take what comes to you. You see, your wise inner self knows the ideal revenue for your business for this year. Just allow it to come into focus, like a number appearing on a screen. Write it here:

My Revenue Target: _____

Now, take another deep breath and let the number settle in. Accept it. We're going to use this to inspire your thinking. This isn't a performance measure. This isn't a goal that's meant to pressure you. It is simply a target, one that is going to inspire breakthrough thinking and new creativity, for you and for your business.

When Deanne asked herself these questions, the number came to her quickly. "It's time for me to crack six figures. I've been working toward this for a few years, my message has become really clear, and I'm passionate about it. It's time to step out, take center stage and be visible in a much bigger way. Making $100,000 would symbolize this for me."

STEP 4: Brainstorm Your Earning Plan

Next we are going to sketch out all the ways you could generate this income. In Chapter 2 you've already designed your ideal services. Now we are going use that information to envision your ideal mix of services and the income they could generate.

Again we are going to use a slightly different approach, a mind map. Mind Mapping was invented by Tony Buzan in the 1970's as a way to engage whole brain thinking. It can be a powerful tool for outlining your business revenue. It allows you to stay in touch with your intuitive knowing (right hemisphere) as you drill down and get specific about your numbers (left hemisphere). This approach unleashes a high level of innovative thinking and forges a potent intention.

Before I learned this approach, I'd get confused and even paralyzed as soon as I tried to imagine how I'd generate the income I wanted. As I'd start to put numbers on the page, a nattering, negative voice began analyzing, double guessing and questioning my ideas. Soon I'd be so discouraged that I'd just stop. I'd fall into passively hoping that something would happen and the revenue would just come in. On the other hand, when I use mind mapping to envision my earning plan, each idea ignites another new idea, and soon they're snowballing. By the time I've finished the first draft, there's an integrated wholeness to the plan, and I'm uplifted, inspired and clear about how this could unfold.

YOUR TURN – STEP 4: Your Earning Plan

We'll use a series of lines and circles to draw a mind map that sketch out a picture of all your revenue streams. Do this in pencil so you can easily adjust and play with it. Keep it light, playful and in the spirit of "What if…?" You can always revise it later. Allow your imagination and intuition to guide you. Quite often, people report that completely new ideas emerge as they work with their mind map.

Start by drawing a circle in the middle of the page, about 2 to 3 inches in diameter. In the circle, write the name of your business and your revenue target for the year (from Step 3). Deanne's looked like this:

Your Revenue Streams

Next, flip back to pages 76 and 77 where you designed your ideal services and jot them down here for easy reference. Your ideal services are your top revenue streams.

My Ideal Services:

_____

_____

_____

_____

As Deanne stated her revenue streams she felt both a tingle of excitement and a twinge of vulnerability. "It's taking some daring and willingness to stretch myself and lay out what I most want to have happen. But I'm getting excited about how great this could be." Her ideal services are keynote speaking, workshops to the public, speakers retreats, product sales (book and audios). When she sketches them on her Money Map, it looks like this:

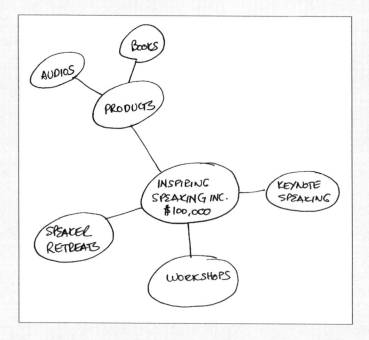

Next, you'll envision the revenue you'd like to generate from each of these services. Consider your first ideal service. If this year went very well, how much business do you want this service to generate? What's your basic unit and average fee? How many of these units do you want this year?

Deanne's first revenue stream is keynote speaking. "While the fee might vary from gig to gig, ideally I want to generate an average of $1500 for each engagement. I speak in three kinds of venues—events with Chambers of Commerce, keynotes through Leading Women Speaking Bureau, and talks at non-profit organizations in the health-care field." When she brainstorms what she really wants to create with keynote speaking this year it looks like this:

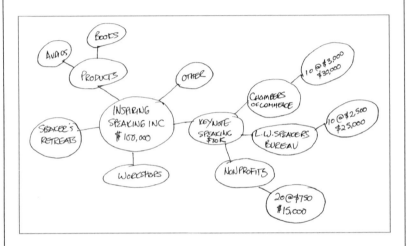

Start with your first revenue stream and ask yourself what you want to generate. Sketch it on your mind map. Draw a line about 2 inches long coming out from the center, just like a spoke comes out from the hub of a wheel, then draw a circle on the end of this line. Write the name of the revenue stream in the circle. Put the dollar figure for the revenue you want to generate. Continue walking through each of your revenue streams, mapping out your ideal scenario from each one. Ask yourself, If this year went very well, what amount of business do I want to do in each? What's my basic unit and average fee?

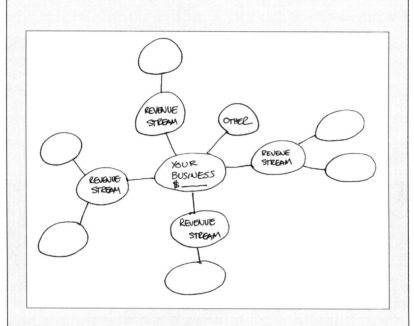

Stay with it until you experience a "click." At some point you will have a felt sense that this gels, it makes sense, you feel excited about what's possible. Leave one branch of your Mind Map open as "Other." Symbolically, this invites the universe to bring revenue to you in ways you can't even imagine right now.

Deanne brainstormed ideas on her mind map, and gave her imagination free rein. She played with different combinations until she felt the "click." Her final mind map looks like this:

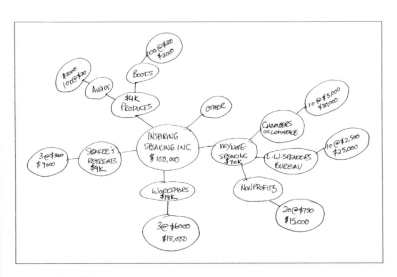

Your Earning Plan

Well done! If you've mapped out your revenue streams with each of your ideal services you've accomplished a lot. This will give you all the information you'll need for the earning plan section of your Money Map. When Deanne finished her Earning Plan it gelled like this:

Deanne's Earning Plan

Keynote Speaking	$70,000		
• Chamber of Commerce Events		10@ $3,000	$30,000
• Leading Women Speakers Bureau		10@ $2,500	25,000
• Non-profit organizations		20@ $750	15,000
Workshops	$18,000	3@$6,000	18,000
Speakers Retreats	$9,000	3@$3,000	9,000
Products: Book	$2,000	100@$20	2,000
Audios	$2,000	100@$20	2,000
Total			**$101,000**

STEP 5: Pull all the Information Together into a Money Map

If you've walked through these first four steps you've hit a milestone. You now have a clearer sense of your personal financial needs and pinpointed your salary. You've outlined your business' financial needs. You've tapped into your inspiring income target. You've brainstormed an abundance of ways you could generate this revenue.

Now, we want to pull this wealth of information into your Money Map in a simple, focused way, so that it becomes an effective tool for leading your business to profitability.

 YOUR TURN—STEP 5: Assemble Your Money Map

Without making this complex, map out your numbers on a one-page Money Map. You can customize the accounts to reflect your unique business design. Plug in your targeted income by revenue stream and by month. Input your projected expenses by month. If you're not comfortable with the results, play around with them until you create a blueprint for the success you want, and have felt that "click" of knowing this is doable.

Deanne's final Money Map looked like this.

INSPIRING SPEAKER, INC.
Money Map 20XX (January to June)   **6 months**

EARNING PLAN

Keynote Speaking	$35,000
Public Workshops	9,000.00
Speakers' Retreats	4,500.00
Product Sales: Book	1,000.00
Audios	1,000.00
TOTAL REVENUE	**$50,500**

EXPENSES	
Basic	
Admin & Finance (accounting, bank chgs, VA)	$2,490
Automoble (gas, oil, insurance, R&M, parking)	3,960
Computer & Office (computer supplies, internet, cell phone, office rent, office supplies)	2,550
Marketing (website, memberships, materials)	1,050
Payroll (salary, critical illness & healthcare insurance)	30,450
Professional development (training, classes, coaching)	1,800
Subtotal Basic Expenses	**$42,300**
Projects	
Book	$3,500
Foundation upgrade (new computer, PDA, etc.)	1,800
Website upgrade	950
Subtotal Projects Expenses	**$6,250**
TOTAL EXPENSES -- January to June	**$48,550**
PROFIT/LOSS	**$1,950**

STEP 6: Embrace the Feelings and "Inner Chatter" This Work Surfaces

I want to let you in on a little-known secret about crafting a Money Map. Doing these steps will most likely trigger a flurry of emotions and inner negative dialogue. Virtually every woman I've coached on mapping out her money plan tells me she experiences a full spectrum of feelings from the elation of possibility to the gut-wrenching despair of self-doubt and fear.

And the secret is, this is a good thing.

Getting specific about money and putting it on paper triggers a lot of strong emotions. It also wakes up our old misconceptions about what is possible and "allowed". For a long time this dynamic stopped me from developing my financial plans, until I understood it is part of the transforming power of authoring a Money Map.

You see, to create something new—grow success and make a difference beyond where you've come so far—will require facing and transforming old, limiting self-concepts and unproductive thinking. If these uncomfortable feelings can't surface, the fears, not you, will start running your business. When you consciously put your numbers on paper as a way to flush up the fear, you will tap into a new source of power and freedom. While at times you might feel challenged by the strong feelings that roll through, know that you are on a path to claiming your real power and achieving the financial success you want.

🖎 YOUR TURN—STEP 6: What Is This Stirring?

What negative chatter, doubts, fears and concerns have surfaced as you start writing your Money Map?

_____

_____

_____

_____

_____

_____

_____

_____

_____

I invite you to embrace those feelings and face the thoughts that surfaced as you craft your plan. A future chapter will equip you with tools to transform this negative chatter. For now, whenever you notice you are feeling anxiety and stress, stop, get curious about your thoughts and emotions, and write them down in your notebook.

STEP 7: Use Your Money Map to Steer Your Business to Prosperity and Profitability

Remember, your Money Map will work its magic only if you use it.

One way of doing this is to set up a regular meeting with yourself to review how your results reflect your plan. You might want to schedule this weekly, or monthly. You might want to do it with your coach, your business support buddy or a trusted advisor. What's important is that you consult your Money Map regularly to gauge how things are rolling out.

✎ *YOUR TURN—STEP 7: Using Your Money Map to Steer You to a Flourishing, Profitable Business*

How will I use this plan? How often will I revisit it? Weekly? Monthly?

_____

_____

_____

_____

_____

_____

Remember, this isn't set in granite. Your plan is meant to be fluid. It is a framework that will morph as you engage in executing your plan. You may have more revenue, or less. More expenses, or fewer. Keep adapting and reworking your plan. Let it become a tool that focuses your intention and steers your business toward success and fulfillment.

If you've worked through each of these seven steps, you've done something awesome! You've translated your vision into a financial roadmap. You've been brave enough to paint a picture of succeeding financially. You've developed a guide that will help you make decisions wisely. You've faced and embraced the resistance that could have held you back. You've quite likely started to tap into a new power in relation to money, and put yourself on a path to flourishing financially and having money serve your greater mission.

Now will we will look at the final—and most transforming—question to ignite extraordinary results in your business.

A Money Map is a tool for translating your business vision into a financial blueprint for a thriving and profitable business. Clarity leads to power -- as you take charge of the financial side of your business, you will attract more opportunities, people and prosperity. Getting specific about numbers can be challenging because it stirs emotions and negative thinking. When you are brave enough to embrace this resistance you can address the issues before they undermine your success. You can create a meaningful and potent money map with the skills you have now. Start first by defining your personal financial needs, and then determine your business' financial requirements. When you map out your best thinking about the revenue you want to generate and how, it creates breakthrough thinking. When you use your Money Map to steer your business, you have the compass points to take your business to fulfillment and profitability.

WHO IS THIS CALLING ME TO BECOME?

Who Is this Calling Me to Become?

"Being in business is not just about making money.
It is a way to become who you are." —Paul Hawkins

This brings us to the seventh question to ignite extraordinary results in your business. It's one that is rarely talked about in traditional business planning, and is really the secret to having your VisionPlan translate into reality. For this dream to happen, who will you need to be? Who is this vision calling you to become?

When I ask a client this question for the first time, there is usually dead silence and I can almost hear her thinking "What the heck did you just say?" You see, most business planning focuses on *what* we want (our vision and goals) and *how* we'll do it (our strategies and actions). But to accomplish our dream these alone aren't enough, no matter how well they're defined. What makes the difference between failure and success is *you*, who *you* will be. There's one thing I know for sure: setting out to achieve an inspiring, compelling vision means finding your essence and becoming who you are, deep down.

Born with Greatness, and Grow Into It

Think about it for a moment. Bring to mind a dream you've accomplished in the past. Who did it call you to *be*? I imagine achieving that dream had an almost magical effect. It unleashed something that was deep inside you, your truest self. Whenever we dare to dream, we dare ourselves to tap into our greatness in a new way. It's like we're becoming who we really are by growing into our true unique self.

One of my most striking experiences of this came in the midst of a very difficult time in my life. I'd been traversing a dark night of the soul for a few years, healing old issues, recovering my inner foundation and taking stock of my true passions. As I came to understand my truest gifts, I decided to look into professional coach training. During an introductory class, the teleclass leader asked us about our vision of ourselves as a coach. Immediately tears welled up in my eyes and my breathing almost stopped. In a flash, I saw myself as the coach I aspired to be. It wasn't a picture in my mind; it was a sense that reverberated through every cell of my body. It was the oddest experience. On one hand, I had an unmistakable understanding: *this is who I am*. It's who I'd been since birth. I'd connected with the hard-wiring in my heart and soul. And, at the same time, I was having a glimpse into my future. This is who I was becoming. When the class ended, the impact of this experience stayed with me. Unquestionably, I knew who I was in my deepest self, and I started *being* her in my day-to-day life. I walked differently. I was more grounded, confident and self-assured. I thought differently. When issues in my current job flared up, rather than spiralling downward into despair, I asked myself how this could be a learning lab for expressing my essence and developing my talents. I acted differently. I felt a new boldness that helped me make many tough decisions. I knew and trusted my direction and path of personal evolution.

It's a paradox. We are born with this essence, our greatness. It is who we truly are. This moment when we come into being represents the full potential of our magnificence. Our greatness lies within us like a seed, always ready to emerge. But it takes an outer 'work,' something we care deeply about like our business vision and life dream, to activate it.

Kristin, the Personal Trainer who you met in Chapter 3 had a dramatic experience of this. For years, she'd yearned to touch people profoundly and teach them how to make breakthrough changes in their health, but she felt trapped in work that was boring, routine and frustrating. When she uncovered her essence, she realized her true nature is The Adventurer. "This was a kind of awakening, I guess you could say. On one hand I knew it was the truth about me, but it took me a few days to accept it. I was actually scared to admit this was truly me. But when I did, it was like my whole sense of self shifted. I literally thought differently, and started doing things effortlessly that I couldn't even attempt before." Within days she launched a workshop on making transformational changes in weight and fitness. "I couldn't believe how quickly things happened. Even though I feared I was risking the ridicule of my co-workers, I just *knew* this is what I was meant to do and took the plunge. It was amazing. As soon as I started telling people about the series they signed up and the class filled within days. From the first session I knew what to say, and people were eager to engage with me in this deeper work. I'd reclaimed a part of me I'd left behind many years ago, and felt fully alive!"

One of my greatest joys is witnessing this transformation. I've seen it over and over again in thousands of people. Each of us is an acorn that is poised to grow into a magnificent oak tree. But this remarkable potential becomes a tangible expression only in relation to others. When we employ our talents in service to others we become more of who we are truly are. Our passion-business can be one of the most powerful vehicles for this transformative, personal evolution. Daily our challenges, interactions with others and creative projects draw forth our unique potential. As we grow our business, our business makes us evolve.

Sara, the ADD coach, is an inspiring demonstration of how our business can grow who we are. She discovered that her essence was "Dynamo". She loves to make things happen—she is a passionate advocate and a highly creative entrepreneur by nature. However, she felt squelched in her work, so much so that she was suffering from stress-related health issues. "At first, when I looked at who my dream was calling me to become, I felt daunted. It was no mystery why I was feeling so stuck. The facts were right in front of me. I had no way to *be* who I am. But it felt like an impossible leap to take a stand on *being* this Dynamo in my current circumstances." Just tapping into a vision of her true essence started to feed Sara new courage and daring. She took the time to design her business thoughtfully so that it would be a limitless platform for expressing who she really is and using all of her many talents. Step-by-step, within two years, she transitioned from a stultifying work situation to being widely known as an ADD coach for creative entrepreneurs. "Each day is a gem. In the morning I'm writing for new information products. In the afternoon I meet with clients. In the evenings I enjoy my family and take time to play the piano. While I'm still addressing some of the health challenges, living my essence more and more is feeding my healing. And, I believe I've just begun."

Who is your dream calling you to be? Your essence—your passion, talents and values—are the well-spring of your true power. You've created a compelling VisionPlan. Now let's take a few minutes to connect with the you, you are becoming. This sense of your true, deepest self—your optimal self—will literally open up new ways of thinking and acting and unleash a potent guiding energy.

 YOUR TURN—*Your Future Self*

Connecting with a vision of who you are becoming is profoundly empowering. In a few minutes we'll do a visualization to meet your future self. As we envision this future self, keep your focus on inner qualities (rather than outer form). It's the essence and feeling we're most interested in, not the specific content or details. For example, when Kristin went inside to meet her future self, she was most inspired by her calm centeredness and unshakable confidence in talking about transformational change principles, rather than focusing on what clothes she was wearing or the size and shape of the room.

Allow about 20 minutes for this activity. Go to a place where you can relax, and focus all of your attention on yourself. If possible, choose a time of day when your energy is high, and set the stage by doing a few of your favourite things that relax and energize you. As part of preparing, I suggest you read over your notes about your essence, your values, your life and business vision and your greater mission.

When you're ready, sit in a comfortable position. Take a few deep breaths to help you shift your attention to your inner world.

Imagine that you are in one of your favourite places in nature, one that immediately relaxes you. Take a deep breath and drink in the beauty around you. Let it touch all your senses. Enjoy the sounds and smells, and notice a few details that bring you joy. The way the light falls on the trees, the movement of the wind, the sound of birds.

Now, turn your head to the right and notice a path. This is your optimal life path, one that's leading to your extraordinary future. When you're ready, get up and start walking along the path. What is it like? You might feel safe, calm, almost protected. Or, perhaps you feel a sense of anticipation, or curiosity.

Around a corner, you see someone emerging and walking towards you. It's your future self, you sometime in the future. You've become so much more of who you really are. You've embodied your truest potential. You're radiating your essence and you're being your passionate, fully expressed self.

Take a moment to notice, what kind of person is this? What is different about her from your present-day self?

Now, shift your perspective and become this person. Notice how it feels to be inside your future self. How does she see the world? What are her strengths? Her qualities? How does she carry herself? If possible, experience in your body where you feel these strengths. Feel the power and presence of this future self, and allow these sensations to register in your body. Your deep inner wisdom is learning from your future self and gaining a blueprint for your journey, an inner compass of 'being' that will guide you from where you are now to realizing this potential.

When you're ready, bring yourself back into present time. Take a gentle breath, and feel your feet on the floor. Remember, this future self is always within you, always available no matter what is going on in your day-to-day life. Take another energizing breath, and when you feel ready wiggle your fingers and toes and come back into the present moment. Take a few minutes to write down your experience.

216 GIVE YOUR DREAM A PLAN

What did you notice about your future self? What qualities radiated most? What is different about her from your present-day self? What did you learn about your true potential?

_____

_____

_____

_____

_____

_____

_____

Your business and life dream is calling you to become your truest, deepest self. I invite you to start *being* your essence in your day-to-day life now. Let the presence you've just connected with in your visualization open up a new way of being, thinking and of acting starting today.

Take Charge of Your Inner Game

Along with tapping into and orienting around your essence, there is another, equally important, aspect of becoming who you're called to be. As you step up to live your highest aspirations and start taking action on your VisionPlan, quite likely you'll encounter something you've felt many times before.

Resistance. Whenever we venture forth to create something new, we encounter inner resistance. Conflicting beliefs that hold us back. Negative chatter that erodes our confidence. Doubts and indecisiveness that undermine our clarity. Rumbling anxiety that prevents us from boldly fulfilling our plans.

How we deal with this resistance determines whether we become our magnificent potential and achieve our greatest possibilities, or are derailed, defeated and never touch our personal magic. This is the inner game of business.

I first learned about the inner game from my Dad. As a child, one of my greatest pleasures was walking around the golf course with him as he shared tips about the art of golf. One lesson in particular stood out. "It's all about the inner game. To succeed, you've got to master your inner game." At the age of 10 it didn't make much sense to me, but I could tell there was a secret buried in his words that I wanted to understand. Gradually I unravelled the mystery: our thinking, beliefs, emotions, imagination and choices either derail us resulting in failure, or propel us forward to extraordinary results.

It's the same in our business. Just like for an elite athlete, our inner game—our mindset and our heart-set—makes the difference between acting from our greatness and achieving our true potential, or always wondering if we have what it takes to succeed with our business dream. Think about it. When faced with adversity, why do some of us become mired in despair and give up, while others of us move forward whatever circumstances happen? The difference is how we play our inner game. There are many potential derailers, however I've seen in myself and my clients that four are deadly if left untended: self-limiting beliefs, critical self-talk, doubt and fear. When an unexpected challenge knocks the wind out of the sails of your dream, can you turn around the inner naysayer? Can you shift from debilitating doubt to soul-deep confidence? Can you feel fear and not be stopped? When you learn to confront these head on and develop practices for transforming them, you will become unstoppable.

The four core practices of the inner game of business are:
• Transforming your self-limiting beliefs
• Breaking free of the inner naysayer
• Tapping into the power of your inner coach
• Using fear to grow your courage

It's vital to learn and use these practices daily in your business. They will equip you not only to deal with inner resistance, but to transform it into new power, confidence, clarity and courage. Over the next few chapters I'll teach you these practices, and as you use them daily they will make the difference between stalling out or creating extraordinary results. They will build in you the capacity, confidence, decisive insight and unstoppable courage to succeed with your dream.

Let's start with the most foundational—revealing and breaking through your inner glass ceiling.

Who you are *being* is key to having your vision become reality. Just having goals and a game plan isn't enough. To accomplish your dream you'll need to become who you are deep down inside. It's a paradox. You are born with your essence *and* you grow into it. You are an acorn poised to become a magnificent oak tree. You stimulate, call forth and express this seed-potential through your outer 'works,' in relation to others. Your passion-business can be a tremendously powerful vehicle for this personal transformation. As you grow your business, your business grows you. Connecting with a vision of who you are becoming—your future self—is profoundly empowering. You can start *being* your truest self now, which literally opens up new ways of thinking and acting, and will guide you to your extraordinary future. Along with expressing your essence there is another, equally important, aspect to becoming who you are deep down—taking charge of your inner game. Your inner game is how you deal with resistance—self-limiting beliefs, negative thinking, debilitating doubts and paralyzing fear—and use it to grow and evolve. Just like for an elite athlete, your inner game—your mindset and your heart-set—will make *the* difference between getting derailed and creating something extraordinary. The four practices that help you take charge of your inner game are: transforming your self-limiting beliefs, breaking free of the inner naysayer, tapping into the power of your inner coach, and using fear to grow your courage

Break Through Your Inner Glass Ceiling

"Whether you say you can, or
you say you cannot, you are right."
—Henry Ford

Have you noticed as soon as we get serious about our dream, something happens? Suddenly all the reasons surface about why we can't do it, why we'll never succeed, or why we're being unrealistic to even dare to think we could do this.

You probably know this dance intimately. Stop for a moment and check it out. Pull out your vision and reread it. Take a moment to imagine it's *really* coming true. What's happening? I bet you're hearing "Yes, but...." Or you're feeling a sinking sensation as a little voice says, "Who are you kidding?"

You've hit your inner glass ceiling—your current self-image and belief structure that have shaped the life you're living now. To build something new, to go beyond where you are, will mean releasing the ways you're keeping yourself small. It will take breaking through self-limiting messages and authoring beliefs that unleash your true potential. Just like a snake sheds its skin as it matures, you'll need to shed the self-image and beliefs that no longer serve who you really are and your dream.

This is the first practice of the inner game of business—transforming unproductive, self-limiting beliefs. When it comes to making rapid, positive change toward our dream, nothing is more important than our beliefs. Nothing.

I'm talking here about all the assumptions and interpretations we've made about ourselves, about others, or about the world at some point in our lives. They can be messages we've absorbed unconsciously from others—our parents, teachers, bosses, mentors, the media, our culture. They may originate as automatic decisions we've made at emotionally charged moments in our lives, as a way to protect ourselves. While they served a needed and useful purpose in that moment, they've long since outgrown their usefulness and now are constricting and restraining our full potential.

Beliefs in themselves aren't inherently wrong; in fact, some of our beliefs are important allies. They allow us to function effectively in life without continually re-thinking and re-learning routine functions. However, most of us aren't even aware of the belief structures that form our sense of self and shape our actions. We fail to tap into our full magnificence because of an invisible glass ceiling, formed by our unconscious, outgrown beliefs. In very real ways it limits who we're allowing ourselves to be.

It is vitally important for the success of your business and for the fulfilment of your dream that you develop the ability to transform these inaccurate, limiting beliefs as a regular practice.

5 Steps to Break Through Your Inner Glass Ceiling

You can shatter your inner glass ceiling and release new potential by taking five steps:
- Discover the self-limiting belief;
- Understand its roots;
- Reveal the evidence that's holding it in place;
- Shift the belief;
- Act to make it real.

First I'll give a quick overview of the steps, and then we'll use them to break through one of your most debilitating beliefs. As we do, I'll share how these steps made a pivotal difference in transforming paralyzing beliefs about marketing that almost sabotaged my dream.

STEP 1: Discover the belief.

Your first task is to surface your hidden self-limiting beliefs. Beliefs are so embedded in our sense of self and our view of life that often it's challenging even to recognize them. A simple way of revealing unconscious messages is to state your vision boldly and listen for any crippling messages that spring to mind and pull the plug on your confidence.

When I first launched my practice, I knew I'd run headlong into my glass ceiling about marketing. Though I was enthusiastic and inspired, I just wasn't following through on letting people know about my services. If things didn't change, I might as well close the doors immediately and get a job. I knew in my heart I was *meant* to live this dream, and had a sense that unconscious, undermining thoughts were at the root of my inaction. But what were they? To unearth them I crystallized my dream in a vivid, simple statement:

"I, Barbara Richards, am creating a thriving coaching business and attracting a steady flow of wonderful clients at $5,000 a month now."

As soon as I finished declaring my intent, a stabbing message emerged. *"You aren't a marketer. You never have been. You never will be. Give up now."* I'd hit pay dirt! This previously unspoken message had stopped me my whole life. If I could shed this image of myself, everything would be different, permanently.

 YOUR TURN—Break Through Your Inner Glass Ceiling

Take a deep breath and relax. All this 5-step process requires is about a half an hour, a piece of paper and pencil, and a sincere willingness to liberate your true potential. Choose a time when you can focus on yourself and your success. I suggest you read through all five steps to get a sense of where we're headed, then dive into transforming a belief that's been stopping you in your tracks and is threatening the success of your dream.

Begin by pulling out your business vision. Read it over and let the exciting possibilities fill your imagination. Once you're feeling the excitement of your dream, capture it in a short sentence. Make it as vivid and juicy as possible! Put all of your heart's desire into a clear statement of intention.

Then, take a couple of calming breaths and become aware of the thoughts running through your mind. What messages have surfaced that pull the plug on your confidence?

Read them over, and notice which statement has the strongest hold on you. Have you hit pay dirt? Is this your glass ceiling? If so, use the following steps to help you shatter it once and for all.

STEP 2: Uncover the Roots

The next step is to examine where this self-limiting belief came from. There are many potential sources—our parents, the media, teachers, mentors—however, the most deeply entrenched assumptions usually start as a decision we made at an emotionally charged moment in the past as a way to make sense of our world and help us through a difficult situation.

When I uncovered the message saying "You're not a marketer" I had no idea where it came from. It seemed like I'd always been this way! But when I asked myself "What's the source of this belief?" a memory flashed to mind about the first time I tried selling when I was in high school. I was a member of Junior Achievement, an after-school program for kids interested in learning about business, and it was finally time to set out to sell our product door-to-door. I was excited as we headed out to a local apartment building. I knocked on the first door. When it opened I launched enthusiastically into an invitation to buy our product. Suddenly, the door slammed in my face. I was shocked.

Bewildered. Hurt. Embarrassed.

It was at that moment that my inner protector took charge of the situation and said, *"You're not a marketer. You never have been. You never will be."* It was the perfect message to take care of me. However, this newly installed belief immediately began to shape my decisions and actions with debilitating consequences. Though uncovering this memory was painful, it was a revelation. I had *chosen* this view of myself. I could now remember a time before this incident when I didn't have this self-image. Something in me felt liberated.

 YOUR TURN —Uncover the Roots

What's the source of your self-limiting message? Did you inherit it from your parents? Absorb it from the media? Or did you make a self-protective decision at an emotionally charged moment in the past? Once you identify the source, you'll begin to release yourself from its grip.

Turn to a fresh page in your notebook and divide it into three columns, headed Message, Source and Impact. Write the limiting belief in the Message column. (It's best to start with one belief and work through the steps as a way to learn this skill and feel the full impact of transforming a belief. Later you can work through other any other messages that are holding you back.)

Now, ask yourself, "Where did this belief come from? What impact has it had?" Just allow your wise inner knowing to bring to mind exactly what is right for you to see and know today. Write your insights in the Source and Impact columns.

Message	Source	Impact
(the limiting belief)	(where it came from)	(how this affected me)
————	————	————
————	————	————
————	————	————
————	————	————

My worksheet looked like this:

Message	Source	Impact
You are not a markete	*Junior Achievement incident*	I believed "You are either born a marketer or you aren't. I'm not. I can't. I'll fail.

STEP 3: Reveal the Evidence

Assumptions get so deeply ingrained because over the years we've gathered evidence that seems to prove they're true. This evidence cements the interpretation in place and we begin to think and act as if this is just the way life is. When we reveal this accumulated evidence and understand the role it's played in making the assumption seem like reality, the belief starts to lose its grip. The glass ceiling begins to crack.

When I asked myself how this momentary, protective message had become an entrenched belief, a soul-level sadness swept over me. I saw how much the belief *"I'm not a marketer"* had influenced decisions and determined the actions I took (and didn't take!).

Memories flooded my mind revealing evidence that had been holding this interpretation in place. In my early twenties a career in the Arts came to a crashing halt because I didn't know how to find my next gig (and never dreamed I could learn how). A couple of years later, I turned down the opportunity to buy my favourite Yoga studio because I couldn't conceive of being able to market and fill classes. In my mid-thirties my dream of offering workshops for women lasted mere months because I froze with fear at the thought of getting the word out and attracting clients. The impact of believing I wasn't a marketer had pulled me under like a powerful undertow in the ocean. Aborted career paths. Missed financial opportunities. A crippling self-image. Feelings of inadequacy. These were the legacies of an unconscious interpretation I'd made many years ago. The evidence that had held this assumption in place had become crystal clear. Simply seeing it this clearly began to shatter the glass ceiling.

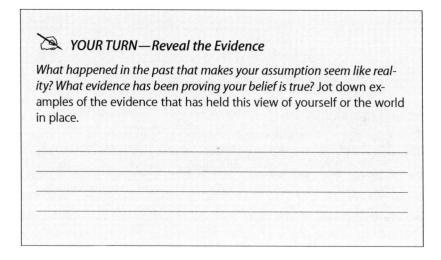

YOUR TURN—Reveal the Evidence

What happened in the past that makes your assumption seem like reality? What evidence has been proving your belief is true? Jot down examples of the evidence that has held this view of yourself or the world in place.

_____

_____

_____

_____

STEP 4: Shift the Belief

To shift a belief permanently, we need to unravel the *facts* from our *interpretations,* and probe past the false assumption to a deeper truth that unleashes our full potential. Just the way we look through clouds to see the expansive blue sky, we look through the limiting belief to find a larger, deeper truth that rings true and unlocks our true potential.

Realizing I'd chosen the self-image of not being a marketer had given me some relief, but I knew if stopped at this point I'd quickly return to old, familiar, unproductive patterns. I was determined to transform this permanently, and resolutely asked myself,

"What's the kernel of fact that seems *so believable* that it's held this view in place for years?" It was tough to untangle fact from interpretation, but gradually the knot unravelled. Yes, it was a fact that I had not made a sale that night long ago in JA (in fact I'd run home, hid all the products under the bed and never tried selling again with JA!). Yes, it was accurate that I'd not pursued certain career opportunities and had prematurely stopped projects because I didn't know how to attract the clients I wanted.

But, suddenly it dawned on me. All the rest was a toxic interpretation. The message *"People are either born marketers or they aren't"* wasn't a fact. It was nonsense! People aren't born marketers. Marketing is a skill, a communication skill. While this might sound obvious to you as you read this, for me, in that moment, it was a revelation. The clouds had given way and I saw a glimpse of the expansive blue sky of possibility.

But for this transformation to be permanent, I knew I needed to go deeper. I challenged the debilitating message *"People are either born marketers or they aren't"* straight on by asking what is *more* true. A whole new view came into focus. It went like this: "Marketing is a communication skill. I'm a strong communicator. I can *learn* this way of communicating called marketing." It was a complete reversal. I was standing in a new place in my life and business. In that moment a new world opened up for me. Something had shifted in the very cells of my body. I felt hopeful and intrigued.

✎ *YOUR TURN—Shift the Belief*

Your inner glass ceiling is cracking, but you are at a crucial point of choice. You can either let your old false interpretation regain control and continue to shape your reality, or you can permanently shift it by digging deeper. Transforming the belief takes separating fact from interpretation, and then thinking bigger, finding the larger, deeper truth that will unleash your full potential.

Take a few deep breaths and mentally and emotionally release every-thing you've done on this so far. Settle into the present moment again. Invite in your wise, knowing self to guide you as we move into trans-forming your limiting belief. Take a look at your belief with fresh eyes. Start separating Fact from Interpretation by asking yourself, "What are the nuggets of fact that makes this message so believable?"

Fact: _____

Fact: _____

Fact: _____

Fact: _____

Interpretation: _____

You'll know when you've separated fact from interpretation because you'll feel a release and new freedom.

My worksheet looked like this:

Fact: I didn't make a sale in JA.
Fact: I didn't know how to get another gig in the film industry.
Fact I didn't buy the yoga studio because I didn't know how to fill classes.
Fact I stopped offering workshops because I didn't know how to at-tract participants.
Interpretation: You're either born a marketer, or you're not. You're not. You're doomed to fail.

Next, go deeper. Ask yourself, "What is more true than this evidence?" Challenge the unproductive belief. Shake it up. Dive into it and dissect it. Think bigger to what is really true. What belief would be productive? What would empower you? What would unlock a whole new level of your potential? Look through the limiting belief to find a larger truth that rings true and write your insights here.

_____

_____

_____

228 GIVE YOUR DREAM A PLAN

> My insight to what was a wider, deeper truth was:
>
> People aren't born marketers. Marketing is a skill, a communication skill. I'm a strong communicator and I can learn the communication skill of marketing.
>
> Once you've written down the deeper truth, stand back and take a breath. Read over your new belief and let it settle in. Are you willing to fully choose and orient around this belief? You'll know you've landed on your deeper truth because you'll feel a new liberation, peace and possibility.

STEP 5: Act to Make it Real

We can only move a breakthrough insight from our head to our emotions through taking action. The way to anchor your new belief and translate it into your new reality is through experimenting, learning and collecting *new* evidence. You'll know when you've tapped into a true, productive belief because it will pull you forward. You'll feel compelled to do things differently.

When my coach challenged me to act in new ways consistent with the new, truer belief I sketched out a list of possible actions I could do in the coming month, and started taking the actions that day. The first piece of new evidence came almost immediately. I attended a networking dinner, and though I still felt nervous about going, everything was different when I got there. I felt relaxed. Rather than feeling pressured to sell people on my services, I focused on naturally connecting with others. That night I met two women who also owned passion-businesses. They were incredibly warm and welcoming. We immediately connected, and they were genuinely interested in my work. Coincidence? Or, new evidence? Over the years, I've continued to challenge myself to learn to market *my* way and I've had a full business and steady flow of wonderful clients for over ten years.

YOUR TURN—Act to Make It Real

Now that you've broken through your inner glass ceiling, there's one more crucial step you'll need to take to make this permanent. You'll need to blow on the flame of this new belief until it takes on a life of its own and becomes your new normal. Just the way in the past evidence held the old belief in place, you'll now need to collect new evidence to anchor your new reality. You'll gather this new evidence through acting in new ways, consistent with this belief being true. Here are a few questions to get you started:

How could I intentionally gather new evidence? How could I step out in a new way, "as if" my new belief is true?

Learning: What learning will grow my mindset and skills consistent with this new belief? What classes, books, mentor, coach will support me in growing my capacity? For example, I took a marketing class, read marketing books and develop my own customized approach to getting the word out about my services.

_____

_____

_____

Actions: What actions will reinforce this new belief and give me more confidence?

For example, I went to a networking meeting immediately and focused on connecting rather than selling.

Action   **When I'll Start**

_____

_____

_____

_____

✵ COACHING TIP

Usually the act of challenging an outdated belief causes a release and transformation. However, sometimes it will require using other practices like therapy, recovery work, EFT, prayer or therapeutic bodywork to fully release and heal the debilitating belief. Do whatever it takes to get free from your self-limiting limiting belief and open space for new choices.

If you've worked through these five steps and broken through your inner glass ceiling, well done! This is tough, deep, often difficult work. And, it's is a vitally important practice. You now have the ability to reveal the outmoded self-image and beliefs that are holding you back. Whenever you encounter your inner glass ceiling, you can use this practice to shed unproductive messages, discover a truer sense of yourself and act in daring new ways. Use this practice regularly to tap into your deep, limitless potential, release a new capacity and become more of your truest self in your life and business.

This first practice of the inner game of business—transforming your self-limiting beliefs—is vitally important. Alone, however, it is not enough, which brings us to the second practice: Redefining how you deal with your inner critical voice.

When you get serious about living your vision, you'll immediately hit your inner glass ceiling—the beliefs and self-image that have shaped the way you are now. Your beliefs are assumptions you've made or absorbed about yourself, others or life in general, as a way to function. Just the way a snake sheds it skin as it matures to create something new, you'll need to shed your outmoded beliefs. It's vitally important to develop the ability to transform your inaccurate beliefs as a regular practice. You can shatter your glass ceiling by discovering the self-limiting belief, understanding its roots, revealing the evidence holding it in place, then shifting the belief and acting to make it real. You can only move a breakthrough insight from your head to your heart by taking action consistent with your new belief. Your beliefs shape your destiny, and you have the innate ability to author your beliefs. Use this practice regularly to shed outmoded beliefs, tap into your limitless potential and become more of your truest self in your business and life.

Break Free of the
Inner Naysayer

*"Never wrestle with a pig. The pig always wins,
you'll both get dirty, and what's more, the pig
will enjoy itself." —Old Texan Saying*

"I just don't know if I have what it takes to succeed in my business." Marie, the Personal Chef, confided. Her breath caught in her throat as she went on to say, "I'm passionate about my vision, but as soon as I start to take the first steps, a wave of doubt rolls in and I start questioning everything."

If you too are hearing a nagging voice of doubt about your vision, I want you to know you aren't alone. As soon as we take steps towards our heart's desires, an inner wrestling match begins. A nattering, critical voice erupts and questions our talents, abilities, motives and even our sanity. (Can you relate?) Surprisingly, it seems that the closer we get to our truest passions and authentic self, the louder and harsher the voice of our inner naysayer becomes.

We all seem to wrestle with this same inner negative voice. While the words of your naysayer might be slightly different from mine, the intent and impact are always the same. It robs us of our trust in ourselves and stops us in our tracks. Most of us would never speak to another person the way we unconsciously speak to ourselves. If we allow this critical voice to be in charge it will erode our confidence and cripple our creative expression. To succeed with our dream, we need to learn to break free of its grip and engage it in a new way.

This is the second core practice of the inner game of business: transforming your relationship with your inner critical voice.

But, how do we do this? Just like the old adage warns us, if we get into a wrestling match with our inner naysayer, it will always triumph and derail us from bringing our unique contribution to the world. So, fighting it isn't the solution. For years I tried to eradicate the inner naysayer, but came to realize this isn't realistic either. The critical voice is part of us and not something that can be eliminated. It's just the way we're wired up as human beings. In fact, it has a role to play. Its job is to protect us from harm, keep us from taking risks, stop us from over exposing ourselves and save us from feeling the stinging bite of failure.

While we can't stop the inner critical voice, we can *choose* how we'll engage with it. Not only is it possible stop the wrestling match, but you can create a radically different relationship with this voice. As unbelievable as it might sound, the inner naysayer can become an ally and a guide that will help you achieve your highest aspirations.

✍ YOUR TURN – Your Inner Naysayer

How is your critical voice eroding your confidence? As you've envisioned your extraordinary future, what has the inner naysayer been saying?

_____

_____

_____

_____

_____

A New Dance

You can transform this wrestling match forever by taking a very different approach. There are three steps I use almost daily that have helped me break free of the strangle hold of negative thinking, claim my inner authority, and forge a new level of personal power:

Listen, don't wrestle;

Take charge. Learn when and how to talk back;

Get the gift.

As we explore these steps, I'll share how they helped me unlock my creative power at a key point in growing my business and transform my naysayer into a vital inner ally.

Listen. Don't wrestle.

Okay, it probably sounds ridiculous to suggest listening to the inner naysayer. Its words carry such a sting, why would we stop to *listen* to it? But it's just like in our relationships with other people. When we stop and listen, I mean really listen with sincere curiosity, something happens. A quiet calm comes over us and we realize these comments aren't reality. They're simply our inner critic's opinions.

A few years ago when I started writing my first website, a paralyzing wrestling match broke out each time I faced the blank page. After a few months of this devastating creative block, I felt desperate. If something didn't change soon I feared I'd never get my work out into the world. One morning as the panicky feelings descended, I decided to stop resisting the knot in my stomach and listen to what the negative voice was saying. A rush of statements poured out. As they came into view, I simply wrote them down. I became genuinely curious and throughout the day I continued to listen and jotted down the negative judgements whenever I heard one.

A remarkable thing happened. By the end of the day, I realized the naysayer was like an old-fashioned juke box. It had only a limited number of tunes to play and when they were done, all it could do was repeat, and repeat, and repeat. I felt liberated! The critic, rather than being a daunting, dominating authority, was actually a scared, vulnerable part of me doing its best to protect me from harm.

YOUR TURN—Break Free of Your Inner Naysayer

Listen. Don't Wrestle.

How is *your* critical voice eroding your confidence? Bring to mind one of your priority projects, one that really matters to you that's stalled out, and use it as your focus as we walk through these steps. Turn to a fresh page in your notebook, and write down a few sentences describing the project and the outcome you'd love to create. Then sit back and listen. What's your inner naysayer saying? Just notice what is going through your mind. Don't judge these thoughts, just take note of them and write them down.

It takes courage to listen to the harsh judgements of the naysayer, but it will be worth the risk. Becoming a witness to your inner naysayer's conversation starts to break its grip. As you go through your day, stop at random times and listen for the spirit-draining thoughts. Then, after you've jotted down the inner critic's chatter, look over your notes, and pull out the top ten most common critical messages.

Top Ten most critical messages about this project

1. _____
2. _____
3. _____
4. _____
5. _____
6. _____
7. _____
8. _____
9. _____
10. _____

Some of mine were:

Who do you think you are? You're no writer.

Anything you have to say has been said before, and much better.

There are thousands of coaches out there. You have nothing unique to offer.

You'll just make a fool of yourself.

You'll never do this.

This will never work.

You'll never succeed.

Anything you'll do will look amateurish.

Take Charge. Learn when and how to talk back.

Now that you've listened to your inner negative voice and heard its criticisms, it's time to take charge. When the comments of our inner naysayer lurk in the shadows out of direct view, we are the unwitting victim of its bullying. However, once we can get the comments into the bright light of day and view them objectively, we have the power to *choose* what to brush aside like a pesky bug and what to challenge and refute.

This insight was a turning point for me in writing my website. For months I'd believed it was the fear of what others would think of my site that was cutting off my creative flow. Gradually it dawned on me. It wasn't the criticism and rejection of others I feared; it was the criticism I was directing at myself. Until I learned to stand for myself, regardless of the outcome of my work, my inner critic would continue to erode my confidence and prevent me from making my contribution.

As I looked over my list of top ten critical comments, I felt a shift. I understood I no longer needed to accept my inner critic's voice as definitive. I could *choose* what to do with these comments. Some criticisms disappeared as soon as I listened to them. Other comments were easily released with a nodding acknowledgement, like saying "Thank you for sharing." Other attacks were exaggerations or outright lies that required me to call the inner critic's bluff and assertively challenge them.

The most debilitating attack on the list was: *You aren't unique. There are thousands of people doing what you do. Give up now.* Each time I heard this statement, it cut to the quick and gutted any sense of motivation, passion and creativity I had. It was a time for me to take charge and talk back with all the courage, conviction and clarity I could rally.

The dialogue went something like this:

"Actually, that's not true. I can see why you say that. It is true that there are now thousands of coaches in the world. And there are thousands of excellent professionals working with people to find their passion and build successful businesses. However, no one does it the way I do. I believe there are people I'm uniquely equipped to serve. I will not give up. I am doing this, and I will continue to do this."

The effect was amazing. My inner naysayer stopped in her tracks. There was a profound silence. We had embarked on an entirely new relationship, adult to adult.

Take Charge. Stand for Yourself.

Look over your list. Which negative comments have already lost their sting just because you've listened to them? Which critical blurts are like pesky bugs that just need to be brushed aside? Which are toxic untruths that must be challenged? Pick one of these statements, and refute it strongly and with conviction:

_____

_____

_____

_____

Get the Gift.

Now that you've established a new adult to adult relationship with your inner critical voice, you can go beyond just neutralizing the negative relationship. Unbelievable as it might sound, you can forge a working partnership with your inner naysayer. It can become an ally in your creative venture. There is a gift of wisdom buried in the tirade of your inner critic. You can un-wrap it by becoming curious about what it's attempting to protect you from, and what it can teach you.

This final step in breaking free of the devastating creative block came when I asked my inner critic two questions I learned from Harriette Klauser, a writing coach: "What are you afraid of?" "What can you teach me?" An unmistakably clear message came back. *"I'm afraid you will make a fool of yourself. I'm afraid you are going too far, too fast. I can teach you to do this at a pace that will not harm you."*

I was stunned. My inner critic knew me extremely well. I *did* have a pattern of taking risks before I was ready and in the past had paid a high price in stress and lost self-confidence. I understood for the first time that, when I listened to the vulnerable part of myself, it would give me valuable information that would guide my efforts with increased self-love and effectiveness. As I dialogued with my inner critic, we designed a step-by-step plan that ensured I wouldn't make a fool of myself, prevented me from over-promising, and gave me more than enough loving support as I stepped out professionally with my website in a bolder and bigger way. I had broken free of the exhausting wrestling match and discovered that my inner critic can be a wellspring of wise information.

Get the Gift:

What nugget of wisdom might be buried in the tirade of your inner critic? Take the dialogue with your naysayer further by asking these two questions, with genuine, compassionate curiosity:

What are you afraid of?

_____

_____

_____

_____

What can you teach me?

_____

_____

_____

_____

Allow the deeper concerns of your vulnerable self to surface, and continue the dialogue as it shares its gift. When you courageously and compassionately listen, your inner naysayer will transform from a paralyzing adversary into a valuable contributor to your creative process.

This new dance will equip you to stop the wrestling match forever. No longer will you be paralyzed in the face of your inner naysayer's harsh judgements. You can now listen, take charge and get the gift that will help you be even more effective in growing your business. You can use this second practice of the inner game of business to break free of the inner naysayer, strengthen your inner authority, and engage your inner naysayer as an ally and guide that helps you achieve your heart's desires.

There's a hidden and profoundly important benefit in transforming your relationship with your inner critical voice. It frees you up to tap into a power and presence that is greater than any challenge or opportunity you will ever face in pursuing your dream. Which brings us to the third core practice of the inner game of business: Finding your Inner Coach.

We *all* have an inner critical voice. If a doubting, negative voice is undermining your confidence, you're not alone. As soon as you take steps towards your heart's desires, a wrestling match with your inner naysayer begins. This inner naysayer has a role to play—to protect you from harm and failure. While you can't stop the nattering voice, you can *choose* how you'll engage with it. Through listening, taking charge and getting its gift you can transform the voice from adversary to ally. There is a gift of wisdom buried in the tirade of your inner naysayer. You can un-wrap it by asking "What are you afraid of?" "What can you teach me?" When you break free of the exhausting wrestling match, you can build an alliance that will help you become even more effective in growing your business.

Tap into the Power
of Your Inner Coach

Each of us has all the wisdom
and knowledge we ever need right within us.
It is available to us through our intuitive
mind, which is our connection with universal
intelligence. —Shakti Gawain

What if you could get answers to your most important business questions simply by asking?

You have within you a power much greater than the inner naysayer. A voice that when listened to will guide you to make decisions and take actions that will always be in your best interest. We call this power by many different names—our wise self, our higher power, our greater self, our gut knowing, our intuition. Whatever we call it, we each have access to an amazing wellspring of wisdom, knowledge, power, practical know-how and love that is far greater than we might be consciously aware of in day-to-day life.

For our purposes, I'm calling this wise, inner partner your Inner Coach. You might already have a powerful, living relationship with this higher aspect of yourself and a name that speaks to you. If so, as you

242 GIVE YOUR DREAM A PLAN

read the next few pages, just replace "Inner Coach" with whatever name makes most sense to you.

As a passion-business owner, one of your most vitally important tasks is to learn to connect with, listen to and act on this knowing. When you develop a partnership with this higher presence, it has seemingly magical effects. This is the third core practice of a powerful inner game—tapping into the power of your Inner Coach.

Your Inner Coach is committed to you realizing the fullest expression of who you are and wants you to succeed beyond what you could possibly imagine at this moment. It can inspire you, champion you and challenge you when you need it, and will love you unconditionally through trials and triumphs. Your Inner Coach is also a no-nonsense motivator who will not tolerate excuses, avoidant behaviour or your favourite defences. It is steadfastly committed to your greatness and will settle for nothing less. Your Inner Coach is tremendously practical, and it can lead you to innovative thinking and inspired action. You can ask for simple guidance in daily life, or you can engage in deep dialogues for breakthrough solutions to long-standing problems. This wisdom and motivation is always available, and you can access it anytime and anywhere.

Just to be clear, it's not necessary for you to believe in a divine presence for this to work. I've found that it is enough to accept that there are aspects within us which are greater than we are normally aware of. It's our greatness. Each of us has in us the potential for more wisdom, love, strength, compassion, creativity and transforming power than we have yet realized. If we believe this is accessible, that is enough to open the connection. If you aren't already accessing the support of your Inner Coach, it's an ability you can learn. In fact, this is a foundation skill you *must* acquire to realize your dreams. Without this compassionate, wise, butt-kicking inner champion, you are like a stand-alone computer, disconnected from the infinite resources of the world-wide web. You risk having fear lead your decisions, and you simply won't have the staying power to weather the challenges of growing your business.

Whenever I start working with a client, my intention is that they cultivate a powerful relationship with their Inner Coach. I urge you to invest in forging an unshakable connection. When you do, you'll pierce through the fog of indecisiveness and find the source of your true power.

There is simply no one else who can do this work for you.

✍ YOUR TURN—Your Inner Coach

When in the past have you connected with your wise self? Have you brought pressing business issues to your inner partner for insight? What real-life experiences of support, motivation and guidance have you had?

Dialogue for Breakthrough

There are many ways to connect with the wisdom of your Inner Coach, and you might already have some that work well for you. If this is new to you, even though your Inner Coach is available at any moment, it's often not easy to know where to start looking. An extremely simple method is to just start a conversation with your Inner Coach, trusting it is there and will answer you. Let me give you an example of how a dialogue with my Inner Coach turned around a seemingly impossible challenge in my business.

A few years ago in late winter, as I reviewed my financial situation and my client portfolio, the exuberant optimism I'd felt in January was fading into frustration bordering on futility. Though I'd taken marketing programs, worked with a marketing coach and grown tremendously, I was still not where I wanted to be. It was time to tell a truth I hadn't yet faced. I pulled out my journal (to be honest, it felt like a desperate, last-resort action), and I decided to give this problem to my Inner Coach for a real dialogue. I spilled out onto the page, and into the presence of my Inner Coach, the fears, frustrations and foreboding that this would never change. When it was all out, I took a deep breath. I felt relief at baring my soul to my Inner Coach and waited to hear what she would say.

A single question came out. "Why do you think it is this way?" It cut to the heart of the matter. What was going on, really? The question opened another floodgate and I emptied my thoughts, speculations and concerns onto the page. And then, once again, waited. A loving yet no-nonsense voice said, "Barbara, I've heard all the things other people have said to you about marketing and attracting clients. But they sound hollow, empty and more like "shoulds". What I want to know is, what do *you* think? What do *you* know for sure about marketing? What do *you* believe is the way for you to attract clients?"

Her question cut right through my swirling fog of confusion. In a flash, I saw a clear picture of my model for marketing. I immediately started to draw a picture of my marketing funnel and sketched out a compelling vision of actions. A deep, calm, knowing confidence welled up inside. This moment proved to be a turning point in my practice. Never again did I question my marketing abilities. Never again was I at a loss for what to do to attract clients. Through asking for, listening to, and being willing to act on the guidance of my Inner Coach, I'd broken through and found my own unique, effective and doable marketing approach. (If you're interested in reading more about this, I've written about it extensively on my blog at visionworkcoaching.com/blog.)

There are many ways to connect with the wisdom of your Inner Coach, and if you have one that works well for you I encourage you to use it now to get answers to your most pressing business issues. If this is new to you, in a moment we'll use a brief visualization and writing activity that has helped many people access their wellspring of wisdom.

In time, as you develop an unshakable bond with your Inner Coach, you'll find yourself having breakthrough dialogues without having to pause to visualize and write. You'll frame a specific business problem, and then spontaneously dialogue with your Inner Coach while you're walking, relaxing or even in the midst of business interactions.

 YOUR TURN—Dialogue for Breakthrough with Your Inner Coach.

Let's begin by assuming that you have within you a source of understanding that knows who you are, what you have been, and what you can most meaningfully become in the future. This source knows all about your business, its true reason for being and the contribution the world needs from it. This inner presence can help direct you in very immediate and practical ways toward achieving your dreams and purposes.

Bring to mind the specific business concern you jotted down a few minutes ago. Open your notebook to a fresh page and in a few words, state your situation simply and honesty, something like:

"I'm stuck with marketing. I haven't taken action in a month."

"I'm excited about my idea about my new service, but I cannot describe it to others."

"My office is piled with paper and loose ends, again. I'm overwhelmed and don't know why it always ends up this way."

"I just lost three clients and I'm afraid my business is falling apart."

"I'm delighted with my new contract, but don't know where to start."

When you're ready, close your eyes and take a few deep, calming breaths. Do whatever helps you shift from the outward pull of busyness to the quiet presence of this moment. Settle into a comfortable sitting position, and turn your attention inward.

In your imagination, go to one of your favourite high-energy places. It might be a sun-drenched beach, or a sanctuary in the forest, or a mountain vista. For a few minutes, just let go and drink in the rich, peaceful energies of this place. Allow them to feed your soul and fuel you right down to the cells of your body.

Now, notice that you hear a sound to your right. As you turn your head, you see your Inner Coach coming into view. Trust your imagination is giving you the perfect image to symbolize your Inner Coach. It might be a woman or a man. It might be an animal, or a symbol like a glowing light or an opening flower. Accept whatever you see, and focus your attention on how it feels to be with your Inner Coach. Allow absolute acceptance, unconditional love, all-embracing compassion, uplifting inspiration and wordless trust surround and embrace you.

Gently, when you're ready, begin a conversation with your Inner Coach just the way you would with a dear, supportive, trusted advisor. Tell your Inner Coach about your most pressing issue. Open your deepest feelings, frustrations and desires. Ask the most compelling question in your mind and heart. Spend as much time as you want in this dialogue.

When it feels right, thank you Inner Coach and say whatever you want to bring this time to a close for now.

In your imagination, go to one of your favourite high-energy places. It might be a sun-drenched beach, or a sanctuary in the forest, or a mountain vista. For a few minutes, just let go and drink in the rich, peaceful energies of this place. Allow them to feed your soul and fuel you right down to the cells of your body.

Now, notice that you hear a sound to your right. As you turn your head, you see your Inner Coach coming into view. Trust your imagination is giving you the perfect image to symbolize your Inner Coach. It might be a woman or a man. It might be an animal, or a symbol like a glowing light or an opening flower. Accept whatever you see, and focus your attention on how it feels to be with your Inner Coach. Allow absolute acceptance, unconditional love, all-embracing compassion, uplifting inspiration and wordless trust surround and embrace you.

Gently, when you're ready, begin a conversation with your Inner Coach just the way you would with a dear, supportive, trusted advisor. Tell your Inner Coach about your most pressing issue. Open your deepest feelings, frustrations and desires. Ask the most compelling question in your mind and heart. Spend as much time as you want in this dialogue.

When it feels right, thank your Inner Coach and say whatever you want to bring this time to a close for now. Bring your awareness back into the present moment, feel your feet and notice the sensations in your body. Open your eyes and turn to a new page in your journal. Immediately write down what became clear to you in this conversation.

What does your Inner Coach look like? What did you ask your Inner Coach?

_____

_____

_____

_____

What did you learn by asking this question? What specific guidance did you receive from your Inner Coach? What's become clear to you?

_____

_____

_____

_____

I strongly urge you to write down what occurred, even if it seems very fuzzy at the start. Often messages and "marching orders" become clearer and clearer as we write them down.

If you've taken the risk of opening up to the love, guidance and no-nonsense practical support of your Inner Coach, well done! Quite likely you've heard the clear voice of wisdom of your inner wise self, and have some concrete insights that are pointing you forward.

Now, act. When we listen and act on the directions of our Inner Coach, our business and life becomes a miraculous journey. However, it takes a special kind of willingness to do this. To forge a living, fruitful relationship with your Inner Coach you must follow through on the directions as quickly as possible. This means acting on what you get without hesitation, without second guessing, controlling or debating. For most of us, it requires tremendous trust to step out into unknown territory and move into action, when we have no guarantee about the outcome.

Which brings us to the fourth practice of the inner game of business: Moving from fear to courage.

You have within you a voice that, when listened to, will guide you in ways that are always in your best interest. The third practice of the inner game of business is accessing the power of your Inner Coach. Your Inner Coach is an amazing well-spring of wisdom, love and practical know-how. This coach within is committed to you being the fullest expression of who you are. Your Inner Coach is unconditionally loving, and a no-nonsense motivator that won't tolerate excuses. You can connect with your Inner Coach simply by starting a conversation and trusting it is there to answer you. When we ask, listen and act on the directions of our Inner Coach our business and life become a miraculous journey.

Use Fear to Grow
Unstoppable Courage

"When you're moving, you're shaking."
—Barbara Sher

"I've been terrified every day of my life
but that's never stopped me from doing
everything I wanted to do."
—Georgia O'Keefe

"I think my plan is wrong," Jessica, the financial planner we met in chapter one, said despondently. "I was so pumped about offering this new workshop, but as soon as it came time to invite people I froze. If I was doing what I'm meant to do, I wouldn't feel that way. I'd feel great, right?"

I used to think the same way—if I was doing what I was meant to do I'd feel fearless, bold, unstoppable. But it just isn't that way. In fact, feelings of vulnerability are a sure-fire indicator that we're on our authentic path and living our dream. Fear is the natural companion of creative action. There's no way around it. Whenever we move toward what matters we feel anxiety, trepidation or outright fear....as well as the exhilaration of taking authentic action.

Creating a new relationship with fear, one where it stops being an enemy and starts being a direct link to our deepest courage, is the fourth practice of the inner game of business.

Fear, more than any other factor, prevents us from boldly living our dreams. Most of us have absorbed distorted notions about fear. *"I shouldn't be feeling afraid. If I do, something is wrong with me." "Having fear is a sign of weakness." "If I feel fear I can't take action. I'll have to wait until I feel better."* The low rumble of anxiety keeps us from hearing our guidance. It often has us choose one path for our business rather than the one we truly want. It stifles our creativity, blocks us from opportunities and keep us trapped in a life that is simply too small.

To make your VisionPlan a living, breathing reality, you'll need to learn to embrace and dance with fear in a new way. When you become more masterful with fear, you'll discover the secret that all accomplished women know. Beyond fear, there is an energy that will help you make a positive difference in the world.

✍ YOUR TURN—Where Is Fear Stopping You?

How is your life currently limited by fear? What are you holding back on in your business? If you had double the courage, what would you do that you're not doing currently?

_____

_____

_____

_____

_____

_____

From Fear to Courage

The key to breaking the paralyzing effect of fear is to begin to respect it. We need to learn to decode its message and understand when to listen to it, and when to take action even in the face of discomfort.

At times fear can indeed be signaling there's real danger in sight. For example, maybe you really *aren't* ready to take this action. Perhaps this project *isn't* financially viable. Possibly, the partner you're considering working with *isn't* reliable. In these cases, fear is alerting you that the cost of the action you're considering taking will be just too high emotionally, financially or socially, and it's vitally important that you listen to it. According to Gavin de Becker, a renown security expert who consults with governments, organizations and individuals on safety issues, true fear is a survival signal that sounds only in the presence of danger. It's nature's built-in guidance system. When we accept this survival signal, welcome its message and listen, fear is an effective tool we can use to our benefit.

However most of us confuse true fear with the butterflies. Usually the anxiety that we let stop us is an automatic self-protective reaction, one that sneaks up on us when we're stepping into the unknown. Every time we try anything new, anything that summons our greatness and stretches our capabilities, we feel the jitters and nervousness of healthy anxiety. This fear—butterflies about the unknown—visits us all, and can't harm us.

Letting the whispering voice of this fear stop you, however, can damage your dreams. You must learn to challenge this fear and wake up from its trance. Becoming masterful with fear involves increasing your tolerance of discomfort and strengthening your ability to take action in the midst of feeling queasy, quaking and unsure. When you do, you'll access your true power, the power it takes to make your vision a reality. Courage.

You have, right now, access to a power that is far greater than any feelings of trepidation. You can learn to tap into this wellspring of bravery and use it to move you beyond paralyzing discomfort.

Grow Your Courage Muscles

Courage isn't a bold, brash, daring feeling. In fact, it's more than a feeling. Courage is an energy, an attitude, a *choice* that we can bring to any situation. It is a quiet expression of the heart. Our real power to embrace and move through fear springs from love. When we're willing to feel anxiety and act anyway, we tap into the unstoppable power of our deepest courage which Stephen Gaskin describes so beautifully:

"It means that you see the importance of the thing in front of you so strong, and you care about it so much, that even if your knees are knocking like castanets, it doesn't matter. You love enough…that it's worth your while to do it."

The way to become masterful in the dance with anxiety, to grow your courage muscles, is to feel your feelings, endure the discomfort, observe your resistance and go for it anyway. Each time you face a fear and take action, you gain more courage. Just the way you build your physical strength at the gym, you build your courage by practice, practice, practice. The more you work with fear, the more your confidence will grow.

I want to offer you a simple yet profoundly powerful way to use fear to build courage every day—The Risk a Day Game. The rules of the game are very straight forward. From this day forward, choose to stretch yourself on a daily basis. Every day, actually seek out opportunities to face your fear and take action.

This had a life-altering effect for me. Before I learned this approach, I was a kind of "binge and bust" person when it came to tackling challenging actions, and this played out most strikingly with marketing. Marketing triggered a paralyzing fear for me. I'd become inspired about the possibilities for my business and lay out marketing actions, but I'd set Mount Everest sized expectations and freeze with fear. Inaction would cascade into paralysis, and then I'd slide into a pit of doubt and just stop moving. After a few days my mood would shift and I'd start flirting once more with my soul's vision, and the cycle would repeat. I'd accomplish a few actions, but they took a such a high toll on my self-esteem I knew if I didn't find a new way, I would be incapable of succeeding in living my soul purpose.

The Risk a Day Game changed this pattern forever. When a mentor coach shared with me how she'd used the Risk a Day Game for years, I knew immediately I'd found the secret. Each day I challenged myself to take one scary step toward my dream that triggered feelings of anxiety. Playing this daily game proved to be the turning point in my business moving from a "someday dream" to a fulfilling reality. No more giant expectations. No more doldrums of paralyzed inactivity. No more binge and bust cycles. I played the game whole-heartedly and gradually tapped into an unstoppable core of courage.

 YOUR TURN—Playing the Risk a Day Game.

Use the Risk a Day Game to train yourself to become someone who naturally wants to face fear instead of someone who avoids it. From this day forward, actively look for opportunities to face your fear by taking one action that moves you out of your comfort zone. I'm not suggesting parachuting out of a plane or driving a race car. What we're looking for is even bigger—taking authentic actions that move you closer to who you're meant to be.

Each day, choose at least one item from your Action Projects, one that challenges you to stretch beyond what feels comfortable. For example, Marie the Personal Chef set out her daily risk as sharing her services with one new person. She picks up the phone and calls a prospective client, or puts on her Chef Jacket when she goes to the market to help spark conversations. Deanne, the speaker and author, challenges herself to write new material in her authentic voice for two hours a day, rather than simply re-using her standard corporate presentations. Shelley, the Executive Communication Coach, promises herself that she'll state clearly to her new assistant what she wants, then address any resulting conflict directly and with heart.

Your daily risk will be unique to you, and it will vary from day to day. You might reach out to new person, attend a new group, make a tough decision, risk being vulnerable in a relationship, or step up to a new level of leadership. How will you know what action to take? Listen to your gut. Listen to your Inner Coach. Listen for your marching orders for today. You'll know if it's a true stretch because you'll feel both the tingle of excitement and the jitters of fear. The key is to choose a doable action, one that is out of your zone of comfort and yet one you know you're ready to take.

Take a deep breath, and pause for a moment. If just the notion of designing a daily engagement with fear has triggered some trepidation, breathe, notice it, and keep going. Pull out your Action Projects and read over your action maps. When you're ready, invite in your Inner Coach. Ask yourself the following questions and quickly jot down the insights that come to you about your risk for today.

What's the next step toward living my dream? What have I been avoiding that I know it's time to do?

Check: Is this doable? Can you take this action today? If not, give some more thought to this until you land on an action that, even though it might take your breath away, you know you can act on it. Now, pick a time today when you will do it.

Challenging your anxiety about the unknown and acting anyway opens a door to freedom. No longer will you be hostage to your moods, bound up in avoiding discomfort, waiting until you "feel up to it." You have the tools to create a new relationship with fear and to access the true power it takes to make your dream a reality—your deepest courage.

Most of us have distorted notions about fear that prevent us from boldly living our dream. We think feeling fear means there's something wrong, or we aren't ready. In fact fear is the natural companion of creative action. Feelings of vulnerability are a sure-fire indicator that you're on your authentic path. Quite likely to make your VisionPlan a living reality you'll need to learn to dance with fear in a new way. The key to breaking the paralyzing effect of fear is to decode its message – is this real danger, or the butterflies? Beyond fear is an energy that is far greater than trepidation: courage. Courage is a choice you can bring to any situation. True courage springs from your love. Each time you face a fear and take action anyway you will gain courage. You can build unstoppable courage by daily taking at least one risk, an authentic action toward your dream. When you challenge your anxiety and take action anyway, you open a door to freedom, courage and your true power to make a positive difference.

You now know the four core practices of the inner game of business. They will equip you to face business highs and business lows and boldly stride toward your dream. No matter what resistance occurs, you can deal with it in a way that grows your capacity, confidence, decisive insight and unstoppable courage. I invite you to take on the challenge of mastering your inner game and being one of the people who touches their personal magic and creates extraordinary results.

LIVING YOUR VISIONPLAN

Living Your VisionPlan

"When we dare to dream, we dare
ourselves to grow into our greatness."
—*Barbara Richards*

We began this book by saying your dream matters. It's vitally important that you claim your passion and bring your unique, valuable and needed contribution to the world. We've come full circle, and now you know the seven questions that ignite extraordinary results and unlock your power to turn your dream into reality.

If you've worked through these questions chapter by chapter quite likely you've re-awakened your vision, unleashed your passion, and tapped into your inspiring life and business dream. You know *what* you want, *how* you're going to accomplish it, and *who* you're becoming as you grow a business (and life!) you love. You have a roadmap that will take you where you're meant to go.

I wrote this book to give you the tools, strategies and support to live an authentic, passionate life and grow a business you love. I've wanted my words to inspire, empower and challenge you to dig deep, unleash your magnificence and live your highest aspirations. Now it's up to you to make these plans *real*. No matter how well crafted, these plans are only as good as you make them.

And that depends on one thing. Taking the next right step.

When we boil it all down, there is really only one thing we do, again and again. We take the next authentic action. Living your VisionPlan is like walking a path on a foggy day. You can't see the entire path ahead, but you can always see the very next step. Once you take it, the next one appears.

It's the same thing with your business. You see, it's impossible for you to know today exactly how your wonderful dream will occur. You can trust however that when you take the next step, another one will be revealed. The path will open up and the people, resources and opportunities will come to you as you take the next action toward your dream. Whenever you feel stuck, rather than getting derailed, ask yourself: "What's my desired outcome? Where am I now, really? What's my immediate next step?" And then take it.

These actions are rarely dramatic, demanding leaps. Most often they are small, doable tasks, but always related to the heart of your vision. These purposeful actions, done day in and day out, week after week, year by year will add up to extraordinary results in your business and a profound personal transformation in your life.

I challenge you to make your VisionPlan a living reality. Courageously listen to your deepest commitments and bravely walk your soul's path. Live your dream of an extraordinary life, one where every day you express your passion, make a meaningful difference that matters to you, and feel soul-level happiness and fulfillment.

I'd love to hear your success stories or questions as you develop and live your VisionPlan. Please feel free to send me an email at barbara@visionworkcoaching.com or share them with me on my blog *Passion, Purpose & Profit* at www.VisionworkCoaching.com/blog. I'd love to post your successes (of course with your permission) to inspire others to follow their business dream and learn from your successes.

I hope we have the opportunity to meet some day and that you'll share your story of living your dream.

Until then, make your one wild and precious life count.

Acknowledgements

I've heard it said many times that it takes a village to raise a child, and through writing this book I've discovered it also took a community for me to find my voice and get my message out into the world.

I am deeply grateful to Barbara Sher, who has put legs under *my* dreams since 1979 when her book *WishCraft* literally fell off a bookstore shelf into my hands. It was the turning point in becoming a practical dreamer. In January 2005 Barbara came back into my life when she launched her WriteSpeak group, which opened the way for fulfilling this life dream —writing my first book. Thank you Barbara for connecting me with my "orphan" and believing I have a message worth sharing.

Eternal gratitude to Matthew Pearl whose brilliant editing transformed my rambling thoughts into the book I envisioned, and more. Your writing coaching revealed the "gold," inspired me to keep going, and grew my confidence to express it.

Heartfelt admiration and appreciation to Linda Naiman (Creativity at Work, www.creativityatwork.com) whose gift of creative alchemy transformed my plain text into a living book, and visual gem. Collaborating with you is a pleasure.

Over the years I've had the privilege of working with many gifted coaches, and I thank each one of you for your transformational support. Special thanks to: Thomas J. Leonard, (founder of Coach University, www.coachu.com), who turned my raw gifts into a real profession and my dream business. Lynne Grodzki, MCC whose first book showed me the life-changing impact a coaching book can have. Jim Horan (founder The One Page Business Plan Company, www.onepagebusinessplan.com) who taught me how to simplify business planning. Amy Ruppert, MCC who has held the vision of this book these last two years ("You're almost there…") and walked by me step-by-step. Reverends Marvin and Kathryn Anderson, whose spiritual direction unlocked my power as a co-creator.

My heartfelt appreciation to all my wonderful clients who've shared their dreams, vulnerabilities, struggles, triumphs and personal transformation. Working with you has taught me what it *really* takes to create a business and life we love, in the midst of it all.

Thank you to my dear friend, writing buddy and book reader Shirley Vollett, PCC. I so appreciate our partnership in this adventure of living from heart and purpose. With this project, thank you for helping me believe in the value of this message and strengthening my courage to go public.

My deep appreciation to my sister and life-long friend, Margaret Spence Krewen, whose daring move to start her passion-business at mid-life continually inspired me to keep writing.

My dear life partner Michael, thank you for listening to me chatter, complain and cheer about how my writing day went each Friday, for supporting me through highs and lows, and for always keeping me laughing.

And, reverent appreciation to the Creative Spirit from whom all blessings flow.

About The Author

Barbara Richards, a coach since 1994, is a pioneer in the coaching profession. She has empowered hundreds of talented independent professionals worldwide launch and grow successful passion-businesses. The practical and transformational questions in *Give Your Dream a Plan* came directly out of the real-life challenges she and her clients face daily.

> *"In my mid-twenties I said a heart-breaking "No." My mentor offered to sell me her Yoga studio, which would be a dream come true. But even though Yoga was my passion and I'd excelled at teaching it for several years, in my heart I knew I didn't have what it would take to succeed in running this business. Passion alone wasn't enough.*
>
> *This started a quest. What does it <u>really</u> take to grow a successful business doing our passion?*
>
> *After more than a decade of experimenting and learning (including two businesses that folded after only a few months) I began to grasp the principles and practices of building a business from the inside out. In 1998 I established my dream business, VisionWork Coaching Services, and I've consistently earned a good livelihood doing what I love ever since. I've grown a business that's aligned with my deepest commitments, and becomes more fulfilling and prosperous each year. It became my mission to share these principles with others."*

As a coach to talented, purpose-led business owners she blends executive coaching with personal leadership development to help clients find their passion, grow a business they love, and live a rich and rewarding life.

Barbara is a passionate advocate of the power of coaching. She holds the highest credential in the coaching profession, Master Certified Coach, and has served as a coaching educator for over a decade as faculty with Coach University (2000) and associate faculty with Royal

Roads University, Graduate Certificate in Executive Coaching (2008). Her work has been covered in articles in the *Globe & Mail* and *Canadian Business*. She loves residing in Vancouver, British Columbia with her husband Michael.

About VisionWork Coaching Group

"Isolation is a dream killer."
— Barbara Sher

The one thing I know about living our vision is that it's more than just reading a book and getting inspired. It's a new way of living and working. At times this can be challenging and if we try to go it alone we usually stall out, or even fail. I want you to have all the support you need to step out boldly and make your dream a living reality. VisionWork Coaching Group offers a range of services that provide inspiring support, leading-edge ideas and practical tools to help you grow yourself and build your business. We work with individuals and groups world-wide via telephone, webinars and in-person workshops.

VisionPlanning™ Coaching via Telephone

Private coaching by telephone will empower you to grow your success your way, at your optimal pace. We'll use the 7 Questions to unlock your deepest desires for your business, map out your roadmap to success and make pivotal changes that will lead to the results you *really* want in your business and your life.

Ignite Extraordinary Results ™ Classes, Retreats and Workshops

In lively teleclasses or in-person events, join with like-minded passion-business owners to design and successfully launch your VisionPlan™. In an accelerated, guided process you'll articulate your compelling vision, and be nourished and become ready to courageously take the next right steps.

We are available to your organization or group to facilitate off-site planning retreats or teleclasses via webinar using the 7 Questions methodology. We will custom design team conversations that map out your future vision, foster deep team alignment and establish new practices for increased productivity.

Private VIP Vision Retreat

As busy business owners, one of our greatest challenges can be taking time out of our demanding schedules to look at the big picture. A VIP Vision Retreat will allow you to step away from the pressures of daily life for a day, and focus entirely on yourself. In a beautiful nature-setting, you'll use the 7 Questions to tap into your business and life vision and map out your inspiring one-year VisionPlan™.

For more information on these services, or to join the Passion & Purpose community please subscribe to Barbara's newsletter *Passion, Purpose & Profit* at:

www.VisionWorkCoaching.com

Made in the USA
Charleston, SC
09 April 2012